REVISE EDEXCEL GCSE
Science
Extension Units
REVISION GUIDE

Series Consultant: Harry Smith
Series Editor: Penny Johnson

Authors: Nigel English, Damian Riddle and Steve Woolley

THE REVISE EDEXCEL SERIES
Available in print or online

Online editions for all titles in the Revise Edexcel series are available Autumn 2012.

Presented on our ActiveLearn platform, you can view the full book and customise it by adding notes, comments and weblinks.

Print editions

Science Extension Units Revision Guide	9781446902677
Science Extension Units Revision Workbook	9781446902585

Online editions

Science Extension Units Revision Guide	9781446904664
Science Extension Units Revision Workbook	9781446904671

Print and online editions are also available for Science (Higher and Foundation) and Additional Science (Higher and Foundation).

This Revision Guide is designed to complement your classroom and home learning, and to help prepare you for the exam. It does not include all the content and skills needed for the complete course. It is designed to work in combination with Edexcel's main GCSE Science 2011 Series.

To find out more visit:
www.pearsonschools.co.uk/edexcelgcsesciencerevision

ALWAYS LEARNING

PEARSON

Contents

A small bit of small print

Target grade ranges are quoted in this book for some of the questions. Students targeting this grade range should be aiming to get most of the marks available. Students targeting a higher grade should be aiming to get all of the marks available.

Edexcel publishes Sample Assessment Material and the Specification on its website. This is the official content and this book should be used in conjunction with it. The questions in *Now try this* have been written to help you practise every topic in the book. Remember: the real exam questions may not look like this.

Rhythms

Many plant and animal responses are controlled by rhythms.

Photoperiodicity

Photoperiodicity or photoperiodism is the response of a plant that changes as day length changes. It is most noticeable in places where day length varies significantly throughout the year.

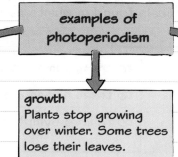

germination
Most seeds are not affected by light as they germinate underground. Some, however, like lettuce, germinate in spring when day length is getting longer. This is usually when conditions for growth are getting better.

examples of photoperiodism

growth
Plants stop growing over winter. Some trees lose their leaves.

reproduction (flowering)
Plants in seasonal areas produce flowers at a particular time of year. Some produce flowers in response to days getting longer (in spring and summer). Other plants flower when day length gets shorter (in autumn).

Circadian rhythms

A circadian rhythm is a pattern of behaviour that changes over a 24-hour period. Circadian rhythms are controlled by an internal biological clock. External factors such as day and night help to match the clock to changes in the environment.

'Circadian' comes from the Latin *circa* meaning 'about' and *dies* meaning 'a day'.

Worked example

The graph shows how a person's need for sleep changes over 24 hours. Sleep pattern normally follows a circadian rhythm. Predict the shape of the graph for the next 24 hours and explain your answer.

The graph should be very like the one shown. This is because a circadian rhythm shows the same pattern of response over about 24 hours.

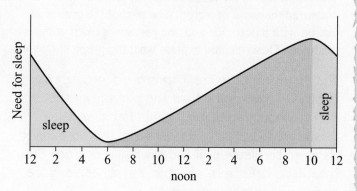

Now try this

target **E-C**

1. Define the terms 'photoperiodicity' and 'circadian rhythm' in your own words.
(2 marks)

target **D-B**

2. Explain why a photoperiodic response during germination is an advantage for plants that grow where there are seasons.
(2 marks)

target **C-A**
HIGHER

3. A person who flies from Mexico to the UK finds it difficult to fall asleep when it goes dark the next night. Explain why.
(3 marks)

Plant defences

Plants protect themselves from attack by producing chemicals. They may make:

- poisons in their cells to deter pests that try to eat them
- chemicals that kill pathogens (such as bacteria and fungi), which infect them and cause disease.

Using plant chemicals

We use some of the defence chemicals found in plants as medicines.

Example	Plant source	Use
quinine	cinchona tree	to treat human disease, e.g. malaria
digoxin	foxglove	to treat human disorders, e.g. heart disorders
aspirin	willow tree and other plants	to relieve symptoms, e.g. pain and fever

You only need to remember the uses, not particular examples.

A 'symptom' is what you feel or show when you have a disease or disorder.

Human food supply

Most of the food we eat comes from plants. Pathogens and pests that attack crop plants cause damage. This reduces the yield of the crop (the amount of food that we can get from the crop).

Worked example

The graph shows the results of an experiment that measured the yield of a crop. One part of the crop was treated with a pesticide and one part was grown without treatment. Describe and explain what the graph shows.

The yield from the treated crop is greater by about 0.7 tonnes/ha than the yield from the crop without pesticide. This is because the pests are killed by the pesticide and so cannot damage the leaves of the plants. Therefore the treated crop plants can photosynthesise more and produce a higher yield.

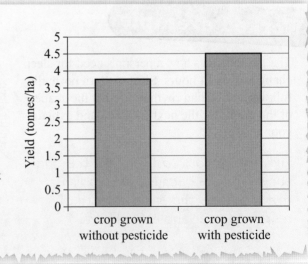

Now try this

1. A person has a headache. Is this a disease, a disorder or a symptom? Explain your answer. **(2 marks)**

2. Explain the advantage to plants of producing chemicals that deter pests or kill pathogens. **(2 marks)**

3. Farmers spend a lot of money on chemicals to kill pathogens and pests of crop plants. Suggest how a farmer might justify this spending. **(3 marks)**

Growing microorganisms

Aseptic techniques

Louis Pasteur carried out experiments showing that once microorganisms are destroyed, they do not suddenly appear again. Microorganisms can only be transferred from something that already contains them, such as the air.

Boiling for an hour kills any microorganisms already in the broth.

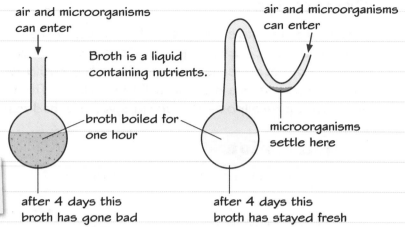

air and microorganisms can enter

Broth is a liquid containing nutrients.

broth boiled for one hour

air and microorganisms can enter

microorganisms settle here

after 4 days this broth has gone bad

after 4 days this broth has stayed fresh

Pasteur's work led to the development of aseptic techniques that are used to destroy microorganisms. These techniques are used to prevent spoilage of food and in surgery (operations) to prevent infection of wounds.

Bacterial growth

The number of bacteria can double every 20 minutes in the right conditions.

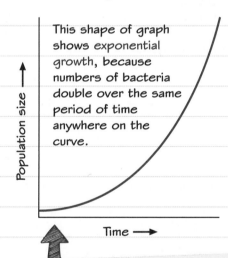

This shape of graph shows exponential growth, because numbers of bacteria double over the same period of time anywhere on the curve.

The rate of population growth will not continue like this because something, such as nutrient supply, will start to limit it.

Worked example

Resazurin dye is blue when there is plenty of oxygen, but turns pink and then colourless as oxygen concentration falls. In an experiment the dye was added to milk in sealed tubes that had been kept at different temperatures for 24 hours. Describe and explain the results shown in the table.

Temperature	Colour
4 °C	blue
20 °C	pale pink
70 °C for 20 s then 20 °C	blue

Oxygen concentration falls because the oxygen is removed from the milk by respiring bacteria. The results show that oxygen concentration falls only in the 20 °C tube. At 20 °C, bacterial growth is rapid. Low temperatures prevent bacteria growing. A brief high temperature kills many bacteria, so milk then kept at 20 °C stays fresh for longer.

Now try this

target D-B

1. Suggest why aseptic techniques are used in surgery. **(2 marks)**

2. Pasteurisation is a process where foods are heated to 70 °C for 20 seconds. Explain why pasteurisation helps to keep food fresh for longer. **(3 marks)**

target C-A
HIGHER

3. Explain how Pasteur's experiment shown at the top of this page led to the idea of aseptic techniques.

(3 marks)

Vaccines

Edward Jenner

Edward Jenner gave a boy a pathogen that causes a mild disease called cowpox. The boy developed cowpox and recovered. Later Jenner gave the boy the pathogen that causes a dangerous disease called smallpox. The boy did not develop smallpox – the cowpox vaccine had made him immune to smallpox.

> Cowpox and smallpox have similar antigens.

Immunisation

Immunisation can protect you from infection.

> Antigens are surface proteins that identify a cell. Antibodies are chemicals made by lymphocytes.

1. A vaccine containing a dead or weakened pathogen is injected into the body. It has antigens on its surface.

2. A type of white blood cell, called a lymphocyte, with an antibody that perfectly fits the antigen is activated.

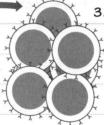

3. This lymphocyte divides over and over again to produce clones of identical lymphocytes.

4. Some of the lymphocytes secrete large amounts of antibodies. The antibodies stick to the antigens and destroy the pathogen. Other lymphocytes remain in the blood as memory lymphocytes, ready to respond immediately if the same antigen ever turns up again.

Worked example

Describe some risks and advantages of immunisation.

Risks:
- Some people get a mild reaction of swelling or soreness, or a mild form of the disease.
- Very rarely a person has a major harmful reaction.

Advantages:
- Immunity is produced without being ill.
- Immunity lasts a long time, often for life.
- If most people are immune, then the few unvaccinated people are also less likely to catch the disease.

Now try this

target E-C

target D-B

1. Describe the difference between a vaccine and immunisation. **(2 marks)**

2. Explain why:
   (a) immunisation can protect you for life **(2 marks)**
   (b) immunisation usually only protects you against one particular disease. **(2 marks)**

target B-A
HIGHER

3. Explain why people who have not been vaccinated against a particular disease are protected if most people are immune to that disease. **(2 marks)**

Antibodies

HIGHER This whole page covers Higher material.

Primary and secondary responses

Worked example

Explain the role of memory lymphocytes in producing the difference in primary and secondary response. Use the graph to help you.

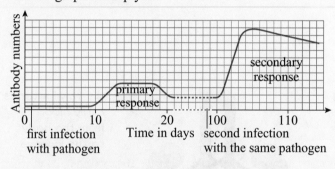

The graph shows that the blood antibody levels are much greater – and the response is much faster – after the second infection compared with the response after the first infection. This is because memory lymphocytes that recognise the pathogen are produced after the first infection and remain in the blood. When the pathogen infects the second time, the memory lymphocytes cause the rapid production of large quantities of antibodies.

Monoclonal antibodies

Monoclonal antibodies are antibodies that carry useful chemical markers or treatments. A set of monoclonal antibodies are identical because they are produced in large quantities from the same hybridoma cells.

B lymphocyte from mouse
- advantage: makes particular antibodies continuously
- disadvantage: B lymphocytes don't divide

cancer cell
- advantage: divides continuously
- disadvantage: doesn't make antibodies

- hybridoma cell formed by fusing a B lymphocyte cell and a cancer cell
- the hybridoma cell divides and produces antibodies that are all the same

Monoclonal antibodies can be used:
- in pregnancy tests to identify if the pregnancy hormone is present in urine
- to stick to blood clots or cancer cells so they can be detected and treated.

Drug and radiotherapy treatments for cancer cannot be targeted precisely and can damage other cells in the body. Using monoclonal antibodies to deliver drugs to target cells means that only the target cells are affected and smaller amounts of the drugs are used.

Now try this

target D-C

1. Explain why using monoclonal antibodies to treat cancer can result in less damage to the body than radiotherapy treatments.
   (2 marks)

target C-A

3. Explain why hybridoma cells must be created in order to produce sufficient amounts of monoclonal antibodies.
   (3 marks)

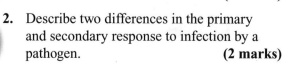
target D-B

2. Describe two differences in the primary and secondary response to infection by a pathogen.   **(2 marks)**

The kidneys

Waste products

Metabolic reactions in the body produce waste products that diffuse into the blood. These substances must be removed to prevent damage to the body.

'Excess' means more than the body can use.

- Carbon dioxide is a waste product of respiration.

- The breakdown of excess amino acids in the liver produces urea.

Structure of the urinary system

the renal veins carry cleaned blood back to the body

Make sure you know the difference between urea and urine, and between ureter and urethra.

the ureters carry urine from the kidneys to the bladder

the bladder stores urine

urine flows through the urethra to the outside of the body

the renal arteries carry blood from the body to the kidneys

the kidneys remove substances including urea from the blood and make urine

a muscle keeps the exit from the bladder closed until we decide to urinate

Worked example

Kidney failure is when both kidneys stop working properly. Toxic urea builds up in the blood and can damage the body. Explain how kidney dialysis or organ donation can help a person with kidney failure lead a more normal life.

In kidney dialysis, blood is passed through a dialysis machine to remove waste urea and excess substances before the blood

is returned to the body. In organ donation, a healthy kidney from another person is placed in the body and connected to the blood system, so that waste substances are removed from the blood.

Kidney dialysis and organ donation are the main treatments for kidney failure.

Now try this

1. (a) State the waste product that is removed from the blood by the kidneys.
   (b) State where this substance is made.
   (2 marks)

2. List the structures of the urinary system that urea passes through, in order, starting with blood in the renal artery. **(2 marks)**

3. Explain why a patient will die if their kidney failure is not treated.
   (2 marks)

Inside the kidneys

Each kidney contains around one million tiny tubules called nephrons. The nephrons make urine.

Nephron structure and function

The nephron is a continuous tubule with several parts. Each part has a different function.

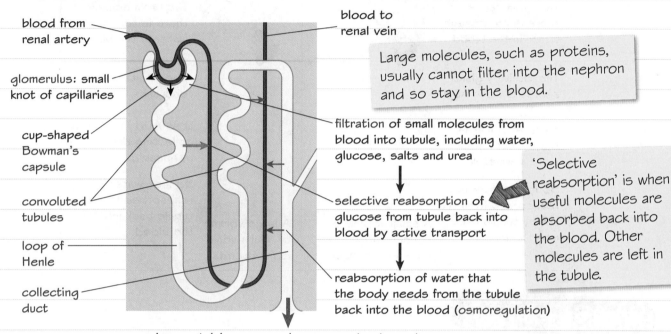

blood from renal artery

glomerulus: small knot of capillaries

cup-shaped Bowman's capsule

convoluted tubules

loop of Henle

collecting duct

blood to renal vein

Large molecules, such as proteins, usually cannot filter into the nephron and so stay in the blood.

filtration of small molecules from blood into tubule, including water, glucose, salts and urea

selective reabsorption of glucose from tubule back into blood by active transport

reabsorption of water that the body needs from the tubule back into the blood (osmoregulation)

'Selective reabsorption' is when useful molecules are absorbed back into the blood. Other molecules are left in the tubule.

urine containing urea and excess water to ureter

Worked example

Explain how the structure of the nephron is related to its functions of forming urine and osmoregulation.

The blood in the glomerulus is under high pressure. The walls of the glomerulus and Bowman's capsule are leaky so small molecules filter from the blood into the capsule. The large surface area of the glomerulus and capsule means filtration happens as quickly as possible. The convoluted tubule and loop of Henle lie close to a capillary, so that glucose and water can be reabsorbed into the blood from the tubule.

Now try this

target **E-C**

1. Describe how the glomerulus and the Bowman's capsule start the process of making urine. **(1 mark)**

target **D-B**

2. Define these terms: **(a)** selective reabsorption and **(b)** osmoregulation.

(2 marks)

target **C-A** HIGHER

3. Urine usually contains urea but no glucose. Explain why.

(3 marks)

The role of ADH

HIGHER This whole page covers Higher material.

The amount of water reabsorbed from the nephrons is controlled by a hormone called anti-diuretic hormone, ADH. This regulates the water content of the blood (osmoregulation).

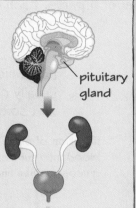
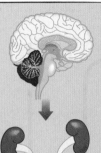

The brain senses there is not enough water in the blood.

The pituitary gland secretes more ADH.

More ADH makes the collecting ducts more permeable.

So more water is reabsorbed from the kidney tubule back into the blood.

A small volume of concentrated urine is produced.

pituitary gland

The brain senses there is too much water in the blood.

The pituitary gland secretes less ADH.

Less ADH makes the collecting ducts less permeable.

So less water is reabsorbed from the tubule back into the blood.

A large volume of dilute urine is produced.

Worked example

Explain what is meant by a negative feedback mechanism, using ADH production as an example.

An increase in blood water content causes the pituitary gland to secrete less ADH. This causes less water to be reabsorbed by the collecting duct in the kidneys so more water is excreted by the kidneys. A decrease in blood water content causes the pituitary gland to secrete more ADH, which causes less water to be excreted by the kidneys. This is a negative feedback mechanism because a change in blood water content causes an opposite change that restores the 'normal' blood water content.

There are other negative feedback mechanisms in the body, but they all show the same feature – a change in the system causes the opposite change to happen to restore a 'normal' level.

Now try this

target D-C

1. State where ADH is produced and its target organ. **(2 marks)**

target C-A

2. Blood samples were taken from a person half an hour after they had been exercising and again after they had drunk a large glass of water. Which sample contained the most ADH? Explain your answer. **(3 marks)**

target B-A

3. Explain why negative feedback mechanisms are important to the body. **(2 marks)**

The menstrual cycle

Between puberty and about the age of 50, women have a menstrual cycle that occurs about every 28 days. During the cycle, changes take place in the ovaries and the uterus.

If fertilisation does occur, then the uterus lining is maintained and menstruation does not happen.

Menstruation is the breakdown of the uterus lining. It begins on day 1 of the cycle and usually lasts between 4 and 7 days.

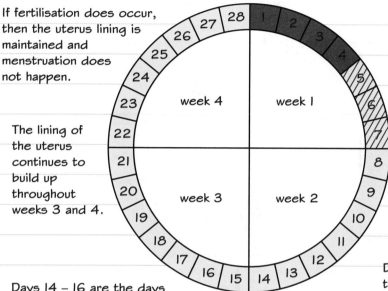

The lining of the uterus continues to build up throughout weeks 3 and 4.

Oestrogen and progesterone are two of the hormones that control the menstrual cycle.

During the second week, the lining of the uterus is gradually built up.

Days 14 – 16 are the days when fertilisation is most likely to take place.

Ovulation is the release of an egg from an ovary. This usually takes place around day 14.

Worked example

Explain why the uterus lining is maintained if fertilisation occurs.

The embryo that develops from a fertilised egg needs to embed in the thick uterus lining, so that it can get nutrients from the mother.

Now try this

target
E-C

1. State which two of the following hormones help to control the menstrual cycle: adrenaline, progesterone, ADH, oestrogen, insulin. **(2 marks)**

target
C-A

HIGHER

3. Explain why failure to menstruate may be the first sign of pregnancy. **(2 marks)**

target
D-C

2. State the day(s) of the menstrual cycle when the following occur:
   (a) ovulation
   (b) menstruation
   (c) uterus lining thickening. **(3 marks)**

Hormone control

HIGHER This whole page covers Higher material.

Four hormones control the menstrual cycle: oestrogen, progesterone, FSH and LH.

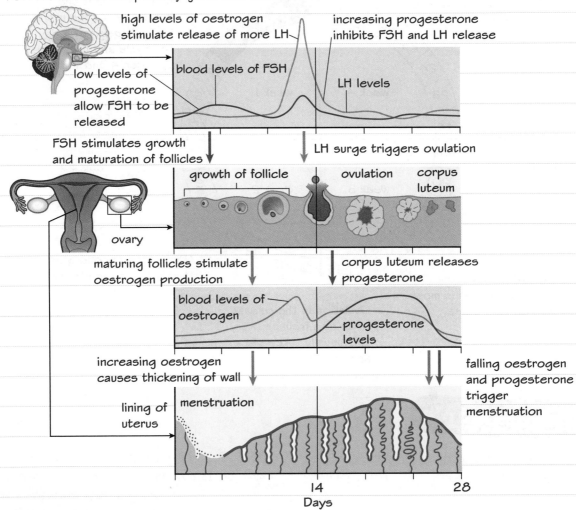

FSH and LH from the pituitary gland near the brain

high levels of oestrogen stimulate release of more LH

increasing progesterone inhibits FSH and LH release

low levels of progesterone allow FSH to be released

blood levels of FSH

LH levels

FSH stimulates growth and maturation of follicles

LH surge triggers ovulation

growth of follicle

ovulation

corpus luteum

ovary

maturing follicles stimulate oestrogen production

corpus luteum releases progesterone

blood levels of oestrogen

progesterone levels

increasing oestrogen causes thickening of wall

falling oestrogen and progesterone trigger menstruation

lining of uterus

menstruation

14   28
Days

Worked example

Explain how the control of the menstrual cycle is a negative feedback mechanism.

Changes caused by the release of one hormone inhibit the secretion of other hormones. For example, progesterone inhibits FSH and LH.

Now try this

target
D-C

1. State where the following hormones are made in the human body:
   (a) oestrogen and progesterone
   (b) FSH and LH.   (2 marks)

2. State what hormonal changes cause menstruation.   (1 mark)
target
C-B

target
C-A

3. State the role of the following hormones in the menstrual cycle:
   (a) oestrogen
   (b) progesterone
   (c) FSH
   (d) LH.   (4 marks)

Fertilisation

Sperm cells and egg cells are adapted to their function.

cytoplasm contains nutrients that the embryo will use to grow and develop

haploid nucleus contains one set of genetic material

acrosome containing enzymes to digest a way into the egg

haploid nucleus contains one set of genetic material

middle section containing mitochondria that release energy from respiration to power tail

cell membrane changes immediately after fertilisation to block entry of other sperm

tail for swimming

Egg cell

Sperm cell

Infertility treatments

Infertility (the inability of a couple to have children) can be treated in several ways.

In vitro fertilisation (IVF)	Egg donation
Egg cells taken from the woman's ovaries are mixed with sperm cells from the man in a dish. One or two healthy embryos are placed in the woman's uterus to develop.	Eggs from another woman are fertilised by the man's sperm using IVF. One or two healthy embryos are placed in the uterus of the woman in the couple to develop.
✓ Useful if a man produces only a few healthy sperm.	✓ Used when woman of the couple has no eggs in her ovaries.
✗ IVF babies may be born early, which can cause problems at birth or later in life.	✗ Hormones used to collect eggs may cause a bad reaction. The egg donor may want access to the child.
Surrogate mother	Hormones
Eggs and sperm from the couple are mixed in a Petri dish. A healthy embryo is placed in the uterus of another woman – the surrogate mother – to develop.	The woman is given extra hormones to help her ovaries release eggs.
✓ Used when the woman of the couple cannot grow an embryo in her uterus.	✓ Used when the woman's hormones are not enough to cause ovulation.
✗ Some surrogate mothers find it hard to hand over the baby to the couple.	✗ There is a greater risk of having several babies at the same time. These babies tend to be born earlier than normal, which can cause problems at birth or later in life.

Now try this

target D-B

1. Describe the features of the sperm cell that help it reach the egg cell for fertilisation. **(2 marks)**

target C-A
HIGHER

2. Explain why an egg cell is only fertilised by one sperm cell. **(2 marks)**

Sex determination

The sex of a person is controlled by one pair of sex chromosomes:

- The genotype XX produces the female phenotype.
- The genotype XY produces the male phenotype.

> Remember that the genotype is all the genes of the individual. The phenotype is what the individual looks like.

Worked example

Explain the proportions of the different sex chromosomes in the gametes of men and women.

Gametes are haploid because they are produced by meiosis. As the sex chromosomes in a woman's diploid body cell are both X, all the eggs she produces will contain one X chromosome. The sex chromosomes in a man's diploid body cells are XY, so 50% of his sperm will contain one X chromosome and the other 50% will contain one Y chromosome.

We can use a genetic diagram or Punnett square to show that the sex of an individual is determined at fertilisation.

Genetic diagram

parent's phenotypes	male	female
parent's genotypes	XY	XX
gametes	X Y	X X
possible offspring	XX XY XX XY	

Punnett square

		possible female gametes	
		Ⓧ	Ⓧ
possible male gametes	Ⓧ	XX female	XX female
	Ⓨ	XY male	XY male

Both diagrams show that, at fertilisation, there is an equal chance of producing a male or a female:
- 50% male XY: 50% female XX
- ratio of 1 : 1 male : female
- 1 out of 2 chance of either male or female.

> You can usually use either a Punnett square or a genetic diagram to answer a question about inheritance. Use the one that works best for you.

Now try this

1. At which stage is the sex of a baby determined: when the egg is fertilised, as the foetus develops in the womb, or when the baby is born?

(1 mark)

2. A couple have two sons. The woman is pregnant with another child. What is the chance that this child is a girl? Draw a genetic diagram to explain your answer. **(4 marks)**

3. Explain why human eggs all contain one X chromosome.

(2 marks)

target C-A
HIGHER

Sex-linked inheritance

The sex chromosomes, X and Y, are not a matching pair. Males only have one X chromosome. A recessive allele on this chromosome may affect the phenotype if it is not matched by a dominant allele on the Y chromosome. This produces a different pattern of inheritance in men and women, and is said to be sex-linked.

> Remember: all other chromosomes are matching pairs, so you have two alleles for all genes on these other chromosomes.

Haemophilia

Haemophilia is a sex-linked genetic disorder. The alleles for the gene are:

- X^H – allele on the X chromosome that produces normal blood clotting
- X^h – the recessive haemophilia allele that causes poor blood clotting.

There is no gene for haemophilia on the Y chromosome. Boys can only inherit haemophilia if their mother is a haemophiliac or a carrier for the disease.

> For sex-linked inheritance, you must show the X chromosome as well as the allele.

		mother: genotype $X^H X^h$	
	gametes	X^H	X^h
father: genotype $X^H Y$	X^H	$X^H X^H$ female, normal clotting	$X^H X^h$ female, normal clotting (carrier)
	Y	$X^H Y$ male, normal clotting	$X^h Y$ male haemophilia

genotypes and phenotypes of possible offspring

Chance of inheriting haemophilia from a father with normal blood clotting and a carrier mother:
- probability: daughter 0/2, son 1/2
- ratio: daughter 0, son 1 : 1
- percentage: daughter 0%, son 50%

Worked example

The faulty allele that causes red–green colour blindness is recessive to the allele for normal colour vision. Around 8% of men have the condition but less than 0.5% of women. Explain this difference.

The allele that controls red–green colour blindness is only found on the X chromosome. Men inherit the condition from one faulty allele from their mother. Women will only inherit the condition if they get faulty alleles from both parents. This is much less likely.

Now try this

target E-C

1. Explain why men are more likely to have a sex-linked disorder than women.

(2 marks)

target C-A

HIGHER

2. (a) Draw a diagram to show the inheritance of red–green colour blindness from a mother who is a carrier and a father who has normal colour vision. (3 marks)

   (b) Use your diagram to calculate the percentage chance of (i) a daughter and (ii) a son being colour blind. (2 marks)

Biology extended writing 1

To answer an extended writing question successfuly you need to:

✓ use your scientific knowledge to answer the question

✓ organise your answer so that it is logical and well ordered

✓ use full sentences in your writing and make sure that your spelling, punctuation and grammar are correct.

Worked example

Humans reproduce by using gametes. Describe how these gametes are adapted to carry out their function.

(6 marks)

Sample answer 1

Sperm cells are much smaller than egg cells. Both cells contain half the number of chromosomes that are in most other cells. Males make lots of sperm cells. Each sperm has a tail, and it uses this to move along. Egg cells need to be bigger than sperm because they stay in the uterus for a long time, so need to be full of nutrients.

Although it looks quite detailed, this is actually a basic answer. It is very important that you answer the question asked – some of the information here, such as on the size of the cells, doesn't do this. The answer could be improved by using some better scientific language (such as 'haploid') and by giving more features of the two gametes.

Sample answer 2

Sperm and ova are both haploid cells – they contain 23 chromosomes, one of each pair found in body cells. Sperm cells need to move to reach the egg, so they have a tail for propulsion and large numbers of mitochondria to provide the energy they need. When the sperm reaches the egg it needs to break through the cell membrane to fertilise it. To do this, the sperm has digestive enzymes in a section of its head. After one sperm has penetrated the egg, the egg changes its cell membrane so that no other sperm can enter the egg.

This is an excellent answer. There is good use of scientific terminology, such as 'haploid', although the answer could also use the word 'acrosome' to describe the pocket containing enzymes in the sperm cell. The description of the adaptations of the egg is good – the only information lacking is the fact that the egg has a large cytoplasm containing nutrients.

Now try this   HIGHER

1. The hormone ADH is produced in the pituitary gland. Explain how this hormone acts on the body to help maintain the water level of the blood.
(6 marks)

Biology extended writing 2

Worked example

Some parents have concerns about having their children vaccinated against measles, a disease spread by a virus. The graph shows the numbers of children vaccinated against measles and the number of cases of measles in England between 1996 and 2008.

Discuss the concerns about vaccination and why it is important to vaccinate children. **(6 marks)**

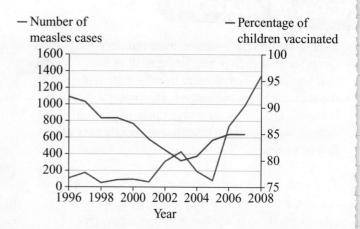

Sample answer 1

The graph shows that the number of cases of measles goes up when fewer children were vaccinated, so vaccination is important. But some parents don't want their children vaccinated because they are worried about bad reactions to the vaccine.

This is a basic answer. There is only a simple interpretation of the graph and only one reason is given why parents might not want their children vaccinated.

Sample answer 2

There was some bad publicity about the measles vaccine causing autism, so some parents stopped having their children vaccinated. But, it turned out that the publicity was not true, but lots of children were not vaccinated so the rate of measles went up – as the graph shows. For immunisation to be effective, a large proportion of the population needs to be vaccinated. In this case, immunisation works by giving children an inactive form of the measles virus, so that they can build up antibodies to the virus.

This is a better answer. The possible link to autism is not required knowledge – but it shows that this candidate knows about possible bad reactions to the vaccine. This is linked to the graph. It is good that the answer says 'some parents' didn't use the vaccine. Some people wrongly think that no children were vaccinated. The answer talks about how a vaccine works, but this is not asked for in the question and so would not gain any marks. To improve, the answer could mention other disadvantages, such as the vaccine not working; and could give more detail about why it is important that a large proportion of the population is vaccinated to prevent measles spreading.

Now try this HIGHER

1. The diagram on page 10 shows the level of four hormones that control the menstrual cycle in humans. Use information from the diagram to describe the roles of these hormones in this process.

(6 marks)

Courtship

Sexual reproduction requires finding and selecting a suitable mate. Behaviour that is used to attract or select a mate is called courtship behaviour.

Worked example

During the breeding season, male red deer (stags) roar at each other. Stronger stags can roar for longer. Female deer usually mate with the stag that roars the longest. Describe what is being advertised by the roaring behaviour, and explain the advantage to male and female deer of this behaviour.

The roaring is a courtship behaviour that advertises the strength of the stag. Males that roar longest will mate with more females and so have more offspring than weaker males. Females can select between males, so that their offspring inherit genes for strength from the male.

In this case the stags are actually stronger, but stronger usually means healthier or better able to survive.

EXAM ALERT!

In a recent question about courtship behaviours only around a quarter of students got full marks. Be clear about which sex is displaying and which is selecting. Usually (but not always) the female does the selecting.

Students have struggled with this topic in recent exams - **be prepared!**   ResultsPlus

Mating strategies

Different animals have different mating strategies.

Some animals:

- mate for life and will only choose another mate if their first mate dies
- have several mates over their lifetime.

Some animals:

- have only one mate for a breeding season
- have several mates for a breeding season.

Note that males and females of the same species may have different mating strategies, e.g. female red deer mate with only one male in each breeding season, but successful red deer stags mate with many females in one breeding season.

Now try this

 target E-C

1. Explain what we mean by courtship behaviour. **(2 marks)**

target D-B

2. Swans have one mate that they stay with for life. Suggest one advantage and one disadvantage of this mating strategy. **(2 marks)**

 target C-A HIGHER

3. Male peacocks use a lot of energy displaying to female peahens. Suggest an advantage for peahens of selecting the male with the best tail display. **(3 marks)**

Parenting

Parenting behaviours

Some animals, particularly birds and mammals, have special behaviours for rearing young. We call these parenting behaviours or parental care. These behaviours include:

- protecting the young from danger
- helping the young to find food
- sheltering the young from cold and wet
- teaching the young new skills, such as hunting.

Evolutionary strategy

A successful evolutionary strategy is one that increases the chance of an individual's genes being passed on from generation to generation.

Parental care can be a successful evolutionary strategy.

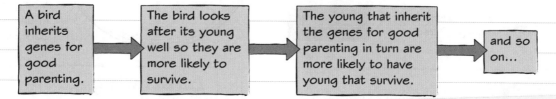

| A bird inherits genes for good parenting. | → | The bird looks after its young well so they are more likely to survive. | → | The young that inherit the genes for good parenting in turn are more likely to have young that survive. | → | and so on... |

In a question about a successful evolutionary strategy, it is not enough just to say that the offspring have a better chance of survival. You need to explain that the parental genes will be passed on from generation to generation.

Worked example

If a fox gets near to the chicks of a bird called a plover, the parent bird will pretend to have a broken wing to attract the fox and will try to lead the fox away from the chicks. Describe a benefit and a risk of this behaviour for the adult plover.

A benefit is that the fox may not see the chicks because it is attracted by the adult. So the chicks will be more likely to survive and pass the parental genes on to the next generation. A risk is that the fox may catch and kill or harm the adult so it cannot look after the chicks.

Now try this

target E-D

1. Explain what is meant by parental care. **(1 mark)**

target D-C

2. Humans have one of the longest parenting periods of any species. Give two examples of parental care behaviour in humans.

(2 marks)

target C-A

HIGHER

3. Cheetahs are large cats that usually hunt on their own. Young cheetahs stay with their mother until they are fully grown.
   (a) Explain the advantage to the young of this behaviour. **(2 marks)**
   (b) State one advantage and one disadvantage to the mother of this behaviour. **(2 marks)**

Simple behaviours

Innate behaviour is behaviour that an animal doesn't have to learn.

Choice chambers

A choice chamber can be used to investigate innate behaviour in small animals.

At the beginning of the experiment five woodlice were put into each chamber.
They were left in these conditions for half an hour.

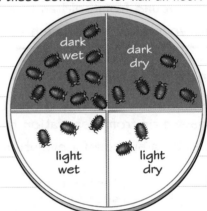

The woodlice move towards the conditions they prefer. This is an innate response.

Woodlice more easily find food and are safer from predators in damp dark places.

EXAM ALERT!

Watch out! In this choice chamber two environmental factors are being tested at the same time: light and water. In a recent question on this, less than 1 in 10 students identified both factors.

Students have struggled with this topic in recent exams - **be prepared!** ResultsPlus

Ethology

Ethology is the study of animal behaviour. Niko Tinbergen was an ethologist who studied the innate behaviour of gull chicks. Gull chicks peck at their parent's beak to ask for food.

He tested different models of adult gull beaks to see which model the chicks would innately respond to and peck at most frequently.

Imprinting

Imprinting is a simple learned behaviour. One example is soon after hatching a gosling (young goose) learns to recognise its mother and will stay close to her. Imprinting only happens at a particular time but may last throughout life without change.

Worked example

Konrad Lorenz was an ethologist who showed that newly hatched goslings could imprint on an object rather than their mother goose if they saw the object first and the mother much later. Explain why this is an example of learning and not innate behaviour.

If recognising the mother was innate, then the goslings would not become attached to the object. Imprinting is a learned behaviour because the goslings learn to recognise what they see first as their parent, and this can be different in different situations.

Now try this

target
E-C

1. Pecking at the parent's beak is an example of innate behaviour in gull chicks. Explain what this means. **(1 mark)**

target
D-B

2. A gosling that is imprinted on an object will not then recognise an adult goose as its parent. Explain why. **(2 marks)**

target
C-A
HIGHER

3. In some bird species the young leave the nest with the mother soon after hatching. Explain why imprinting is a successful evolutionary strategy in these species. **(2 marks)**

Learned behaviour

Habituation

Habituation is a simple form of learned behaviour. It happens when an animal 'switches off' its response to a repeated harmless stimulus. This helps the animal to concentrate on changes in the environment that are important. This is most likely to increase the animal's chance of survival.

Police horses are exposed to crowds during their training so that they learn to become used to the noise. This is an example of habituation.

Classical conditioning

Classical conditioning occurs when an innate behaviour is changed through associating a new stimulus with the old response.

> innate response to normal stimulus
> e.g. salivating when food is present

↓

> added stimulus
> e.g. bell rung when food is presented

↓

> added stimulus is associated with normal stimulus
> e.g. bell associated with food being presented

↓

> conditioned behaviour
> e.g. salivating happens when a bell is rung, even when there is no food

EXAM ALERT!

In a recent question on this, nearly half the students lost a mark because they did not explain that the final stage is only shown when the new stimulus makes the response happen without the presence of the old stimulus.

Students have struggled with this topic in recent exams - **be prepared!**   Results**Plus**

Worked example

Sniffer dogs and dolphins can be trained using operant conditioning. Explain what this means.

Sniffer dogs are often trained with a toy that they enjoy playing with. The first time in training that they find drugs they are given the toy to play with – this happens again and again until the dog will look for the drugs because it knows it will be rewarded with the toy. In operant conditioning, a chance behaviour is strengthened by receiving a reward. At first, the behaviour is chance, but the animal learns to associate the reward with the behaviour and so carry out the behaviour more often.

Now try this

target
E-C

1. A snail that is touched frequently on its antenna will stop withdrawing into its shell. Name the kind of behaviour shown by the snail. **(1 mark)**

target
D-B

2. Explain how operant and classical conditioning are different. **(2 marks)**

target
C-A
HIGHER

3. A rat explores a maze and finds food in one corner. The next time the rat is in the maze it finds the food in the same corner more quickly. What kind of learning is this? Explain your answer. **(2 marks)**

Animal communication

Animals communicate to transmit information to other animals using different types of signals.

Sound	Chemical	Visual
for example: • birds sing to establish and maintain a territory • cats hiss to frighten other cats • deer stags roar to challenge other stags and attract females	animals release hormone-like chemicals called pheromones into the air, e.g. female moths release pheromones to attract male moths	• gestures such as head nodding or hand waving • body language – the position of the body can express feelings and emotion • facial expression, such as showing teeth

Humans show their teeth in smiling, when friendly. Other animals, e.g. chimpanzees, show their teeth as a threat.

Social behaviour

Social behaviour occurs between individuals in a group. It includes the use of different types of signal. Social behaviour can increase the chance of survival of individuals and all of the group, for example, by:

• defending a larger territory
• some individuals watching for danger while others feed
• fighting off predators as a group
• working as a group to hunt for food.

Dian Fossey

Dian Fossey was an ethologist who studied the social behaviour of gorillas by watching them in the wild.

Fossey learned the meaning of many gorilla calls and found that gorillas had complex social relationships. She also showed that gorillas were not violent.

Worked example

Explain how the work of Jane Goodall has contributed to our understanding of chimpanzee behaviour.

Jane Goodall watched chimpanzee groups for many years and recorded what she saw. Her work shows that chimpanzees live in complex family groups that communicate using many different calls. She was the first person to record chimpanzees using tools and hunting as a group to kill other animals.

Now try this

1. State why social behaviour is important for gorillas. **(1 mark)**

2. Give two examples of different types of signal used by humans to communicate and explain information the signals carry. **(2 marks)**

3. Elephants in a herd gather together when they are attacked by lions. Suggest why elephants behave like this. **(2 marks)**

Plant communication

Using chemicals

Plants communicate using chemicals. For example, flowering plants produce scents to attract particular animals, such as some insects. As the animal feeds on nectar at the flower, pollen attaches to the animal and is transported to the next flower the animal feeds on. This mutualistic relationship helps both species to survive.

strong sweet scent attracts moths

scent like rotting flesh attracts carrion flies

Plants also produce chemicals that affect other plants. For example:

- Some produce chemicals from their roots that damage the roots of other plants. This reduces competition for resources such as water and mineral ions.
- Some release chemicals into the air when they are attacked by herbivores, to warn surrounding plants. The warned plants then produce poisons. They only do this when warned as the poisons take a lot of energy to make.

HIGHER

Co-evolution

Co-evolution is evolution (change in characteristics) that is caused in one species by a change in another species.

Plants have co-evolved the shape of their flowers with animal pollinators so that only one or a few species of animal can feed at the flower. This benefits both plant and animal because:

- pollen from the plant's flowers is more likely to be taken to a flower of the same species
- the animal is less likely to have to compete with other animals to get the nectar in the flower.

If the relationship becomes too specialised the populations can become too dependent on each other. If one population crashes the other can be affected.

Worked example   HIGHER

Some plant species that are eaten by herbivores make chemicals that are poisonous. Experiments show that plants growing in areas where there are more herbivores make more poison than plants growing where there are fewer herbivores. Suggest why this happens.

This is an example of co-evolution because where there are many herbivores, the plants that survive and reproduce best have large amounts of poison. So the next generation of plants will inherit the genes for producing lots of poison.

Now try this

target
E–C

target
D–B

1. Describe two examples where plants communicate using chemicals. **(2 marks)**

2. State what is meant by co-evolution.
   (1 mark)

target
B–A*

HIGHER

3. Suggest how a plant co-evolved with carrion flies to produce flowers that smell like rotting flesh. **(3 marks)**

Human evolution

Some of the evidence we have for evolution leading to modern humans (*Homo sapiens*) comes from fossils. These include fossils of bones and teeth.

You do not need to remember details such as brain sizes but you do need to remember the names and the general trends.

Species	Ardi (*Ardipithecus ramidus*)	Lucy (*Australopithecus afarensis*)	*Homo habilis* ('handy man')	*Homo erectus* ('upright man')	*Homo sapiens* ('wise'/modern man)
Height	120 cm	107 cm	< 130 cm	179 cm	wide variety but generally taller than other species
When existed	4.4 million years ago	3.2 million years ago	2.4–1.4 million years ago	1.8–0.5 million years	since c. 200 000 years ago
Brain size	350 cm³	400 cm³	500–600 cm³	850–1100 cm³	approx. 1200 cm³
Other details	tree climber, also walked upright	walked upright, face ape-like	flat face like modern humans, first tool user	long-distance walker, strongly built	user of complex tools

Ardi and Lucy are individual examples of their species. Other examples have been found since they were discovered.

Homo habilis and *Homo erectus* fossils were described by archaeologists from the Leakey family.

Stone tools

Stone tools also give us evidence of human evolution. The earliest stone tools are around 2.4 million years old. Over time more complex tools were made, and a greater range of tool types.

c. 2 million years old a large stone that has had some chips flaked off it, e.g. simple hand axes

c. 40 000 years old made from fine flakes split from larger stones many types of tool made this way, e.g. arrow head, spear head, scraper, knife

Worked example

Explain how stone tools can be dated from their environment.

The amount of radiation in samples of sediment just above and below the layer in which the tools are found can be used to date the sediment and so give a range of dates when the tools were left there.

The stone used to make the tools is much older than the tools, so cannot be used to date when the tool was made.

Now try this

1. Name two sources of evidence used to work out how human-like species have evolved. **(2 marks)**

2. Describe two ways that human-like species have evolved over the past 4.4 million years which can be seen from fossils. **(2 marks)**

3. Suggest what the development of stone tools implies about human evolution over the last 2.5 million years. **(2 marks)**

Human migration

Modern humans are thought to have evolved in Africa around 200 000 years ago. Evidence suggests that some of these humans migrated out of Africa around 60 000 years ago.

Climate change

Climate change has affected human migration:

- In the Ice Age more water was frozen in glaciers and ice caps, so sea levels were much lower. This allowed humans to walk between places that are separated by water today, e.g. from Africa to Asia.
- Low sea levels around 25 000 years ago meant that humans could walk from Siberia in Asia across into North America.
- At the end of the Ice Age, humans migrated north as the land became habitable.

During fertilisation, only the nucleus of a sperm enters the egg, so all the mitochondria in a fertilised egg come from the cytoplasm of the female gamete.

Mitochondrial DNA

Mitochondrial DNA is the DNA found inside mitochondria in cells. It has several features that make it more useful than the DNA in a nucleus for tracking human migration and human evolution.

one nucleus in a cell contains nuclear DNA

many mitochondria in one cell contain mitochondrial DNA

easier to extract than nuclear DNA as more abundant

only passed from mother to child

has a higher mutation rate than nuclear DNA so more differences between people

less likely to degrade in fossils than nuclear DNA

Worked example

The African Eve theory states that all people today can trace their inheritance back to one female who lived in Africa between 130 000 and 200 000 years ago.

Describe how mitochondrial DNA provides evidence for the African Eve theory.

Mitochondrial DNA is passed from mother to child. Differences in mitochondrial DNA are caused by mutations. Analysis of these mutations suggests that all people are related to one female who is referred to as 'African Eve' because she lived in Africa.

Now try this

1. People who lived 60 000 years ago in Africa probably couldn't make boats. Suggest how they moved from Africa to Asia across a region where there is water now. **(2 marks)**

2. Explain why mitochondrial DNA is only inherited from the mother. **(2 marks)**

3. Explain why scientists find it easier to study human evolution using fossils by looking at the mitochondrial DNA rather than the nuclear DNA. **(2 marks)**

Biology extended writing 3

Worked example

The Russian scientist Pavlov conditioned dogs to salivate when a bell was rung. The police also use conditioning to train sniffer dogs to find drugs or explosives.

Compare the type of conditioning used in both cases. **(6 marks)**

Sample answer 1

Pavlov used classical conditioning. Here, the dog is given food as a stimulus when a bell is rung. The dog links the bell with the food and will react even if the food is not given but the bell is rung. With police dogs, the situation is similar, but the dogs are trained by using rewards or punishments. This is known as operant conditioning.

This is a good answer. Both types of conditioning are correctly named, although in both cases the description of the conditioning is not complete. For classical conditioning, there is no indication of what the behaviour is. For operant conditioning, there is no indication of what the rewards are, or how reinforcement can be used. Also, there is no indication of any features in common – this is important in a 'compare' question.

Sample answer 2

Pavlov conditioned his dogs by classical conditioning. He noticed that they salivated when food was shown to them, so he rang a bell when they were fed. The dogs learned to associate the sound of the bell with the food, so they showed the salivation response when the bell was rung, even without the food stimulus. Police dogs are trained by operant conditioning. This is similar to classical conditioning as both involve the animal learning. However, in operant conditioning, the animal learns to link a behaviour with a reward, which is usually food or praise. The dog links the reward with finding the drugs or explosives and the behaviour is encouraged. Sometimes a negative reinforcement can be given in the form of punishment, although most animal trainers find positive reinforcement to be more effective.

This is an excellent answer. The use of scientific language is very good indeed – words like 'stimulus', 'response' and 'reinforcement' are used effectively. There is a good description of Pavlov's experiments with classical conditioning, as well as operant conditioning used for police dogs. The answer also mentions that both forms of conditioning involve learning – a very important point.

Now try this HIGHER

1. Explain how scientists have used mitochondrial DNA to help them develop the theory of evolution.
   (6 marks)

Biotechnology

A natural biomolecule is a molecule made by a living organism. Biotechnology is the alteration of natural biomolecules using science and engineering. Biotechnology is used to provide:

- useful substances, e.g. foods such as cheese and bread, and chemicals such as insulin
- services, e.g. tests for chemical pollutants.

Fermenters

A fermenter is a large vessel used to grow microorganisms that produce biomolecules.

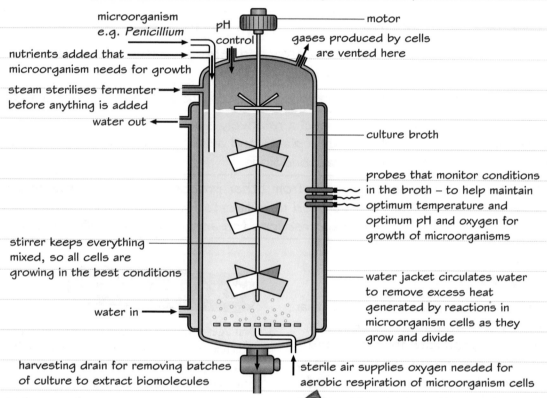

microorganism e.g. *Penicillium*

pH control

motor

gases produced by cells are vented here

nutrients added that microorganism needs for growth

steam sterilises fermenter before anything is added

water out

culture broth

probes that monitor conditions in the broth – to help maintain optimum temperature and optimum pH and oxygen for growth of microorganisms

stirrer keeps everything mixed, so all cells are growing in the best conditions

water in

water jacket circulates water to remove excess heat generated by reactions in microorganism cells as they grow and divide

harvesting drain for removing batches of culture to extract biomolecules

sterile air supplies oxygen needed for aerobic respiration of microorganism cells

Sterilising the fermenter before use and sterilising added nutrients and air are known as aseptic precautions. This stops other microorganisms that might compete with the type being grown from getting into the fermenter culture, which would reduce the amount of biomolecules produced.

Growth of yeast

The rate of growth of yeast can be investigated by measuring the rate that carbon dioxide is produced. This can be used to show that there is an optimum pH for yeast growth.

Worked example

Explain why fermenters are effective for growing microorganisms on a large scale.

Conditions inside the fermenter can be controlled. This means that the microorganisms grow rapidly and the production of biomolecules is as rapid as possible.

Now try this

target E-C

target D-A

1. Insulin is a biomolecule. State what this means. **(1 mark)**

2. Explain why conditions inside the fermenter are continually monitored as the microorganisms grow. **(3 marks)**

3. Explain why the culture in the fermenter is continually stirred.

(3 marks)

Microorganisms for food

Microorganisms are used for making many different kinds of food.

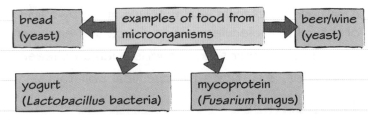

examples of food from microorganisms

bread (yeast)

beer/wine (yeast)

yogurt (*Lactobacillus* bacteria)

mycoprotein (*Fusarium* fungus)

Using microorganisms for food production has advantages over using animals or plants.

Factor	Advantage
rapid population growth	microorganisms grow and reproduce much more quickly than animals or plants
ease of manipulation	microorganisms are easier to handle than whole plants and animals
production independent of climate	fermenters need a relatively small area and can be built almost anywhere, while plants and animals need large areas of particular environmental conditions
use of waste products	waste products from other processes, such as from making flour, can be used as nutrients for growing microorganisms – this is cheaper and reduces the amount of waste disposal needed

Making yogurt

Yogurt is made from milk. It is thicker than milk and tastes different. The speed at which yogurt is produced from milk, and the type of yogurt produced, can change depending on the type of bacteria used, the type of milk used, and the temperature or the pH of the mixture.

EXAM ALERT!

Don't get confused between the production of yogurt and cheese. Yogurt-making bacteria make milk thicken but not separate. Enzymes in cheese-making cause the milk to separate into curds and whey.

Students have struggled with this topic in recent exams - **be prepared!** ResultsPlus

Worked example

Fill in the flow chart to describe the process of making yogurt from milk.

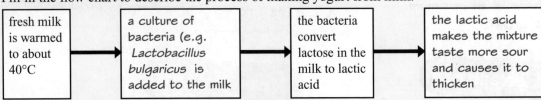

| fresh milk is warmed to about 40°C | → | a culture of bacteria (e.g. *Lactobacillus bulgaricus* is added to the milk | → | the bacteria convert lactose in the milk to lactic acid | → | the lactic acid makes the mixture taste more sour and causes it to thicken |

Now try this

target
E-D

1. Name two foods made using microorganisms. **(2 marks)**

target
D-B

2. Explain why microorganisms can be grown for food almost anywhere. **(2 marks)**

3. Explain why growing food using microorganisms can be better for the environment than growing crop plants or farm animals. **(2 marks)**

Mycoprotein

Mycoprotein is protein-rich food manufactured using the fungus *Fusarium* sp. The fungus is grown in large fermenters.

> This is a short way of saying 'one species of'. It means that the actual species is not important to the description.

Fermenting mycoprotein

The fungus makes long thread-like hyphae, which gives mycoprotein a fibrous texture.

The broth in the fermenter isn't stirred as this would damage the hyphae.

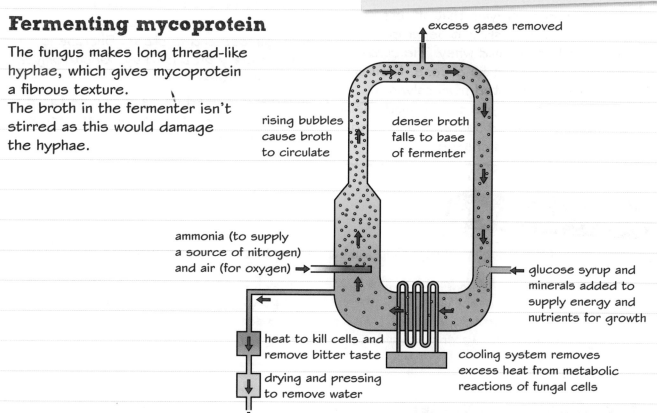

excess gases removed

rising bubbles cause broth to circulate

denser broth falls to base of fermenter

ammonia (to supply a source of nitrogen) and air (for oxygen) ➡

glucose syrup and minerals added to supply energy and nutrients for growth

heat to kill cells and remove bitter taste

cooling system removes excess heat from metabolic reactions of fungal cells

drying and pressing to remove water

mycoprotein ready for packaging

Worked example

Give two reasons why mycoprotein is considered a healthier source of protein than red meat.

Mycoprotein contains no saturated fat, but red meat does. Saturated fat is a risk factor for heart disease, so health advice is to eat less red meat.

Mycoprotein also has a high fibre content, which red meat doesn't. Fibre has many healthy effects. It can reduce the rate of glucose absorption and so reduce glucose and insulin surges, which are thought to increase the risk of type II diabetes. Fibre also moves food through the intestines faster so carcinogens are removed more quickly, reducing the risk of bowel cancer.

Now try this

target E-C

target D-B

1. State what is meant by mycoprotein.
   (1 mark)

2. Explain why a person at risk of heart disease may be advised to replace the red meat in their diet with mycoprotein. **(2 marks)**

3. Describe how mycoprotein is produced. **(4 marks)**

target C-A

HIGHER

Enzyme technology

Enzyme technology is the use of enzymes to make useful products.

Chymosin

Chymosin is an enzyme that affects proteins in milk, making it separate into solid curds and liquid whey. The curds are then used to make cheese. Natural chymosin is extracted from calves' stomachs. The enzyme can be made using genetically modified bacteria, and used to make vegetarian cheese.

Invertase

Invertase (also called sucrase) is the enzyme that converts the sugar sucrose into glucose and fructose. Sucrase is commercially produced by *Saccharomyces cerevisiae* (yeast).

Invertase is used to make sweets taste sweeter and for making the soft centres of some sweets.

Worked example

Identify two types of enzymes used in biological washing powders, and explain why they are used.

Protease enzymes digest proteins and lipases digest fats and oils. Proteins, fats and oils are often found as food stains on clothes. Washing powders with these enzymes work more quickly at lower temperatures than washing powders without enzymes, which saves energy in heating the water and saves time in washing.

Investigating enzymes

Lactase is an enzyme that breaks down lactose sugar. It can be immobilised in alginate beads before it is used to produce lactose-free milk. Immobilising enzymes means that the enzymes can easily be separated from the product so that they can be used again.

- enzyme, e.g. lactase, in sodium alginate solution
- added one drop at a time
- calcium chloride solution
- solutions react to produce calcium alginate beads containing the enzyme – the enzyme is immobilised in the bead

Now try this

target E-C

1. (a) Describe how you can immobilise an enzyme. **(1 mark)**

   (b) State one way that immobilising enzymes is useful. **(1 mark)**

target D-B

2. Invertase (sucrase) is added to a sucrose mixture, which is placed inside a chocolate coat. Describe the change caused by the enzyme that will happen inside the chocolate. **(2 marks)**

target C-A
HIGHER

3. Genetically modified bacteria are used to make chymosin. Explain why this technology is useful. **(2 marks)**

DNA technology

HIGHER This whole page covers Higher material.

Recombinant DNA technology is the use of technology to make genetically modified organisms.

Making human insulin

Human insulin can be made in large quantities from bacteria that have been genetically modified to contain the gene for human insulin.

1　DNA from a human cell is cut into pieces using enzymes called restriction enzymes. These make staggered cuts across the double-stranded DNA, leaving a few unpaired bases at each end, called sticky ends.

2　Bacteria cells contain small circles of DNA called plasmids. The same restriction enzymes are used to cut plasmids open, leaving sticky ends with matching sets of unpaired bases.

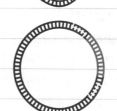

3　The pieces of DNA containing the insulin gene are mixed with the plasmids. The bases in the sticky ends pair up. An enzyme called DNA ligase is added, linking the DNA back into a continuous circle.

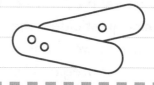

4　The recombinant plasmids are inserted into bacteria. The bacteria can now be grown in huge fermenters, where they make human insulin.

Worked example

Describe the role of enzymes in the formation of genetically modified bacteria.

Restriction enzymes cut the required gene out of the human DNA. They leave 'sticky ends' on the gene. The same restriction enzymes cut open the plasmid, creating matching sticky ends. The DNA ligase enzyme joins the matching sticky ends of the human gene and the plasmid, to make one complete modified plasmid.

EXAM ALERT!

Make sure you are clear what happens in each step of this process. In a recent question on this, only one-quarter of students got full marks. The plasmid must be removed from a bacterium before the gene is inserted. The plasmid is then inserted into another bacterium. The sticky ends allow the insulin gene and the plasmid to join together properly.

Students have struggled with this topic in recent exams - **be prepared!**　ResultsPlus

---

Now try this

target **D-C**

target **D-A**

1. State what is meant by recombinant DNA technology. **(1 mark)**

2. Draw up a bullet point list or a flow chart to show all the stages in producing genetically modified bacteria that make insulin.
(4 marks)

target **C-A**

3. Explain why it is useful to make human insulin using genetically modified bacteria. **(2 marks)**

Global food security

Global food security is the ability to provide enough food for all the people on Earth. As the human population grows, we need to grow more food so there is enough for everyone.

Increasing food production

Conventional plant-breeding programmes can develop new varieties of plants that have higher yields.

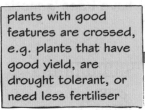

| plants with good features are crossed, e.g. plants that have good yield, are drought tolerant, or need less fertiliser | → | plants grown from seeds of these crosses are selected for their good features and crossed with each other | → | selection and crossing is repeated many times until a high-yielding variety is produced |

Pest management

Pest management strategies can also increase food production by killing the pests that damage crop plants. These strategies include:

- using chemical pheromone traps to attract and kill pests
- using crop varieties that are less attractive to pests
- attracting natural predators of the pests
- using chemical pesticides when pest numbers are high
- rotating crops between different fields to prevent a build up of pests in the soil.

A combination of strategies is usually more successful for controlling pests and less damaging to the environment than just using pesticides.

Biofuels

Worked example

Complete the table to describe some advantages and disadvantages of growing biofuel crops to replace fossil fuels.

Advantages	Disadvantages
biofuels are renewable, fossil fuels are not crop growth takes carbon dioxide from the air	biofuel crops need land to grow on, and this may take land needed for growing food crops

A biofuel is a fuel that is produced from living organisms, such as oil palm trees.

Now try this

target E-C

1. Explain why global food security may become more difficult in the future. **(2 marks)**

target D-B

2. Explain why growing biofuel crops may reduce global food security. **(2 marks)**

target C-A

HIGHER

3. The yield of wheat (in tonnes/hectare) grown in India has tripled over the past 50 years. Suggest two reasons for this. **(2 marks)**

A GM future?

Genetic modification

Plants can be genetically modified using a bacterium called *Agrobacterium tumefaciens* as the vector. For example, the gene for making flavonoid can be inserted into tomato cells to make purple tomatoes.

A 'vector' is something that carries a gene into another cell and inserts it into the DNA of that cell.

Tests have shown that mice with cancer live longer if they eat flavonoids.

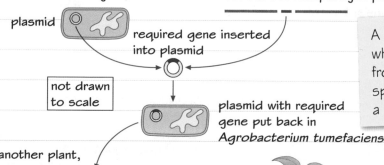

Agrobacterium tumefaciens (bacterium that naturally infects plants and causes crown galls)

plasmid

required gene, e.g. gene for making flavonoid from snapdragon plant

required gene inserted into plasmid

not drawn to scale

plasmid with required gene put back in *Agrobacterium tumefaciens*

A plant like this, which has genes from another species, is called a transgenic plant.

leaf discs from another plant, e.g. tomato, infected with agrobacterium – the plasmid is inserted into the plant's DNA

sections of the leaf discs are used to grow new plants – all cells of the new plants will contain the new gene

---

Worked example

Explain how genetic modification could be used to increase food production.

A gene that helps a plant grow faster or cope better with difficult conditions and produce more seed could be inserted into a crop plant such as wheat. Growing these GM plants would increase the yield of the crop in an area.

Costs and benefits

The genetic modification of crop plants has costs and benefits. These may differ for developed countries, where more people are rich, and developing countries, where more people are poor.

✓ Eating purple tomatoes that contain flavonoids might help anyone with cancer live longer, but they cost more to buy.

✗ GM crop seeds may be too expensive for poor farmers to buy.

Now try this

target E-C

1. (a) Give one example of a transgenic plant. **(1 mark)**
   (b) Suggest one advantage of genetic modification compared with selective breeding to produce a crop plant with a particular characteristic. **(1 mark)**

target D-B

2. 'Golden rice' is a transgenic rice variety that helps prevent blindness in people whose food normally contains little vitamin A. State one cost and one benefit of this development. **(2 marks)**

target C-A

HIGHER

3. Explain why some plants have been genetically modified to produce flavonoids. **(3 marks)**

31

Insect-resistant plants

HIGHER This whole page covers Higher material.

The bacterium *Bacillus thuringiensis* naturally produces a chemical that is poisonous to insect pests such as caterpillars. This chemical is called Bt toxin.

The gene for Bt toxin can be cut out of the bacterial DNA and inserted into the DNA of a plant cell using *Agrobacterium tumefaciens*. Plants grown from these cells produce the Bt toxin. When an insect tries to eat them, the poison kills the insect pest.

> *Agrobacterium tumefaciens* naturally infects plant cells, and so is a useful vector for making transgenic plants.

Using Bt plants

There are advantages and disadvantages of introducing genes for insect resistance into crop plants.

Advantages	Disadvantages
✓ crop damage is reduced so crop yield should increase ✓ less chemical insecticide is needed so other, harmless and useful insects are less likely to be harmed (better for biodiversity)	✗ seed from transgenic plants is more expensive than seed from non-transgenic varieties ✗ insect pests may become resistant to Bt toxin ✗ Bt gene may transfer to closely related wild plants by pollination, which would make those plants resistant to pests too

Worked example

Explain how genetic modification with the Bt toxin gene could increase food production.

Damage to a plant's leaves by an insect pest will reduce the amount of food that a plant makes by photosynthesis. This will reduce the rate of plant growth, including growth of the parts of the plant that we eat. Bt toxin kills insect pests that eat the leaves, so crop yield should increase.

Now try this

1. State why insect-resistant crop plants are less likely to be grown in poorer countries. **(1 mark)**

2. Describe how a wheat plant could be genetically modified to produce Bt toxin. **(5 marks)**

3. Explain how insect-resistant plants could be beneficial to the numbers of animals in a food web. **(3 marks)**

Biology extended writing 4

Worked example

Fermenters like the one in the diagram are used to grow microorganisms on a large scale, both for food and for medicines.

Explain how the conditions in the fermenter are controlled to make sure that the microorganisms are growing at the fastest rate. **(6 marks)**

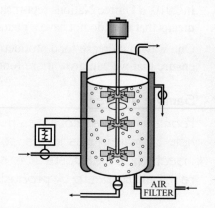

AIR FILTER

Sample answer 1

The most important thing in a fermenter is to make sure that only the right microorganisms grow, so the fermenter is kept sterile. This means careful control of what goes in, as well as thorough cleaning after use. It is also important to make sure that the correct nutrients go into the fermenter so that the microorganisms can keep growing. The stirrers also help to make sure that the nutrients are shared between all the microorganisms.

This is a good answer. There are 6 conditions for fermenters mentioned on the specification – and this answer mentions 3 of them. It also has some good detail about the need for aseptic conditions and about the need for nutrients. However, using the word 'sterile' is not so good – this is not the same as 'aseptic'. Sterile conditions would mean that all microorganisms are killed. To improve, other factors should be mentioned – the most important of which is temperature.

Sample answer 2

It is important to keep the temperature controlled in the fermenter. The microorganisms will respire and raise the temperature, so a cold water jacket is needed to keep the temperature at the correct level. This is also helped by the stirrers. As the stirrers rotate, they circulate nutrients around the fermenter – the level of nutrients added needs to be controlled. The supply of oxygen into the fermenter also needs to be controlled. This is partly because there needs to be a good supply of oxygen for respiration, but also because the air entering the fermenter needs filtering. This ensures that any other microorganisms are removed so that aseptic conditions are maintained. Careful cleaning of the fermenter with steam between uses is essential for aseptic conditions too.

This is an excellent answer. The only factor not mentioned is pH. However, this does not stop this from being a comprehensive answer to the question, with a good level of detail about the features mentioned.

Now try this

1. Describe how enzymes and microorganisms are used in industry to make food for humans.

(6 marks)

Biology extended writing 5

Worked example

In 2010, a United Nations report said that around 2 billion people on the Earth do not have food security. This means that they do not have a guaranteed supply of enough food with the right level of nutrition for health.

One way to increase food production is to use fertilisers. Describe other ways in which scientists can ensure that we can grow more food that contains the right nutrients. **(6 marks)**

Sample answer 1

People in poorer countries need to be able to grow more of their own food. Scientists help by making pesticides, so that the crops grown by farmers do not get destroyed by insects or other pests. It is even possible to genetically modify a plant so that it becomes resistant to pests by producing substances that kill any insects that try to eat it.

This is a basic answer. One reason for this is that it only answers half the question – it could be improved by mentioning ways of growing food with the correct nutritional level. Although it does mention one aspect of GM crop production, there are other types of GM techniques that could be considered, as well as other crop breeding programmes.

Sample answer 2

Scientists can help by producing better crop plants. This can be done by natural methods, such as selective breeding. This involves breeding only those plants with desired characteristics – such as high yield – together. This process is slow, because it needs many generations of plants. A quicker way is to genetically modify the crop plants. For example, the gene for the toxin from *Bacillus thuringiensis* being inserted into crops. The crops make the toxin and are then toxic to insect pests. This may be better than spraying crops with pesticides, as spraying means the pesticide gets into water and soil. GM crops can also be made to improve health. Examples include golden rice, which produces vitamin A when eaten, or crops that are engineered to make flavonoids, which have antioxidant properties.

This is an excellent answer. The topic here is very wide, so there is potentially more detail that could be included in an answer. However, this answer does cover the main areas, both using 'traditional' techniques such as selective breeding and pesticide use, as well as GM technology. It also shows excellent use of scientific language, especially in the use of terms such as 'flavonoids' and 'antioxidants'.

Now try this HIGHER

1. Most people with diabetes need to inject themselves with insulin to control their condition. Describe the processes involved in genetically engineering bacteria to produce human insulin.

   (6 marks)

Water testing

The test for a particular ion should be unique. It must give a positive result with only one type of ion. This way you can be sure which ions are present in a sample.

Qualitative and quantitative testing

> You studied flame tests in Unit C2. Flame tests work on solid samples and samples in solution.

Worked example

State the difference between qualitative analysis and quantitative analysis.

Qualitative analysis investigates the types of substance present in a sample. Quantitative analysis measures the amount of each substance present in a sample.

Flame tests

Flame tests are used to detect certain metal cations. You need to know the flame colours for these metal cations: sodium (yellow), potassium (lilac), calcium (red) and copper (green/blue).

Hydroxide precipitates

You need to be able to describe how to carry out tests for metal cations using sodium hydroxide solution. First dissolve the sample in water, then add a few drops of sodium hydroxide solution. Many metal cations in solution form insoluble precipitates when this is done.

Aluminium ions and calcium ions both produce a white precipitate. You can tell them apart because:

- the aluminium hydroxide precipitate redissolves to form a colourless solution when excess sodium hydroxide solution is added
- the calcium hydroxide precipitate does not redissolve.

You need to know the colours of the hydroxide precipitates for these metal cations: aluminium (white), calcium (white), copper (pale blue), iron(II) (green) and iron(III) (brown).

> Sodium ions and potassium ions are detected using flame tests. Calcium ions and copper(II) ions can be detected using flame tests or hydroxide precipitate tests.

Now try this

target **E–C**

1. What is the difference between qualitative analysis and quantitative analysis? **(2 marks)**

target **D–B**

2. Describe how to carry out tests for copper(II) ions using **(a)** a flame test and **(b)** sodium hydroxide solution. **(4 marks)**

target **C–B**
HIGHER

3. Explain how to distinguish between a sample solution containing aluminium ions and one containing calcium ions. **(2 marks)**

Safe water

Chemists working in the water industry need to test the purity of drinking water. They need to be sure that the water does not contain harmful dissolved substances.

Tests for halide ions

To identify halide ions add a few drops of dilute nitric acid to the sample, then a few drops of silver nitrate solution. A different coloured precipitate forms, depending on the halide ion present: chloride (white), bromide (cream) and iodide (yellow).

'Milk, cream, butter' is one way to remember the colour of silver halide precipitates – silver chloride is white, silver bromide is cream coloured and silver iodide is yellow.

The test for ammonium ions

Worked example

Describe a test to show the presence of ammonium ions, NH_4^+, in a sample solution.

Mix the sample substance with dilute sodium hydroxide solution. Warm it using a Bunsen burner flame. If ammonium ions are present, ammonia gas is given off. Ammonia has a distinctive smell, and it turns damp red litmus paper blue.

The red litmus paper must be damp for the test for ammonia to work.

Worked example

Write a word equation, a balanced equation and an ionic equation for the reaction between silver nitrate solution and sodium chloride solution.

silver nitrate + sodium chloride → silver chloride + sodium nitrate

$AgNO_3(aq) + NaCl(aq) \rightarrow AgCl(s) + NaNO_3(aq)$

$Ag^+(aq) + Cl^-(aq) \rightarrow AgCl(s)$

The state symbol (s) means solid, and it shows that silver chloride is the precipitate.

EXAM ALERT!

An ionic equation usually shows two oppositely charged ions reacting to form a solid product. Make sure that the equation is properly balanced. In a recent exam less than one in ten students achieved any marks on a question on this topic.

Students have struggled with this topic in recent exams - **be prepared!**

Now try this

 1. Describe the tests you would use to identify ammonium chloride. **(4 marks)**

 2. Write an ionic equation to describe the reaction between silver ions and iodide ions. Give the state symbols. **(2 marks)**

Safe limits

The tests that analytical chemists use are based on tests you will have used at school.

Testing water purity

Drinking water is not pure water because it contains dissolved substances. Some of these are deliberately added to tap water:

- chlorine is added to kill harmful microorganisms
- aluminium sulfate is added to remove small solid particles.

It is important to make sure that the amount of each dissolved substance found in drinking water is safe.

Testing blood

Modern blood tests are very sensitive. They can detect and accurately measure very small amounts of substances in the blood.

Analytical chemists test blood samples to help doctors identify why their patients are ill. For example, high levels of aluminium in the blood are linked with Alzheimer's disease.

Worked example

Describe a laboratory test to see if a sample of water contains sulfate ions.

Add a small volume of the water to a test tube. Add a few drops of hydrochloric acid, then a few drops of barium chloride solution. If a white precipitate forms, the water contains sulfate ions.

Tests for carbonate ions

Carbonate ions (CO_3^{2-}) can be tested for using dilute acid. If you add dilute hydrochloric acid to a sample containing carbonate ions, you will briefly see bubbles. The gas is carbon dioxide. It turns limewater milky.

EXAM ALERT!

In a recent exam, many candidates could not balance this equation. Some even showed CO_2 as CO^2 or CO2.

Students have struggled with this topic in recent exams - be prepared!

ResultsPlus

Carbon dioxide is also produced when a weak acid such as ethanoic acid is used. The reaction is useful for removing deposits of calcium carbonate in hard water areas:

$$CaCO_3 + 2CH_3COOH \rightarrow (CH_3COO)_2Ca + H_2O + CO_2$$

Now try this

target
E-C

target
D-B

1. Give two reasons why analytical chemists are employed in hospitals. **(2 marks)**

2. Some drinking water may have become contaminated by aluminium sulfate. Explain why it is important to test the water. **(2 marks)**

3. A stream may have become contaminated by waste from a mine. Describe how you could test the water to see if it contains dissolved iron ions. (You may need to look back at page 35.) **(3 marks)**

Water solutes

Hard water

Water in rivers, lakes and reservoirs may flow over rocks containing calcium or magnesium ions. For example, calcium carbonate is the main compound in the limestone and chalk found in some parts of the country. Some of the calcium or magnesium ions dissolve in the water, forming hard water.

Problems with hard water

Hard water does not easily form a lather when it is mixed with soap. The calcium ions and magnesium ions react with the soap, forming a precipitate. This precipitate is called scum and it causes soap to be wasted.

Calculating concentrations

In a solution, the substance that is dissolved is called the solute. The liquid that dissolves the solute is called the solvent. For example, in sodium chloride solution the solute is sodium chloride and the solvent is water.

EXAM ALERT!

Make sure you say what you would see. In a recent exam, about half of all students did not gain a mark because they did not write about 'lather'.

Students have struggled with this topic in recent exams - **be prepared!** ResultsPlus

The concentration of a solute is measured in $g\ dm^{-3}$ ('grams per cubic decimetre'). You can calculate the concentration of a solute using this equation:

$$\text{concentration (g dm}^{-3}) = \frac{\text{mass of solute (g)}}{\text{volume of solution (dm}^3)}$$

Worked example

250 cm³ of sodium chloride solution contains 1 g of sodium chloride. What is its concentration?
(1 dm³ = 1000 cm³)

Notice how the volume is converted from cm^3 to dm^3 first (by dividing by 1000).

volume of solution in dm³ = 250 ÷ 1000 = 0.25 dm³

concentration = mass of solute ÷ volume of solution = 1 g ÷ 0.25 dm³ = 4 g dm⁻³

Now try this

target E–C

1. (a) Name two metal ions that cause hard water. **(2 marks)**
    (b) 2 dm³ of sodium chloride solution contains 4 g of sodium chloride. Calculate the concentration of the solution. **(2 marks)**

target C–A
HIGHER

2. A 500 cm³ bottle of mineral water contains 0.02 g of dissolved chloride ions. Calculate the concentration of chloride ions in g dm⁻³. **(3 marks)**

Hard and soft water

Temporary hardness

Temporary hardness in water is caused by dissolved calcium hydrogencarbonate $(Ca(HCO_3)_2)$. Temporary hardness can be removed by boiling the water. This works because calcium hydrogencarbonate breaks down when heated. The calcium carbonate formed is not soluble, so its calcium ions cannot react with soap to form scum. Removing hardness from water is called softening.

Permanent hardness

Permanent hardness in water is caused by substances such as calcium sulfate $(CaSO_4)$. Unlike temporary hardness, permanent hardness cannot be removed by boiling the water. Remember that water can contain both types of hardness, so boiling may not remove all the hardness.

Worked example

Ion exchange columns

Use the diagram to help you to explain how water containing permanent hardness is softened using an ion exchange column.

> Ion exchange columns also remove temporary hardness.

The column has little beads in it made from an ion exchange resin. Hard water is sent through the column. As the water goes through, its calcium ions are swapped for sodium ions from the resin. Sodium ions do not form scum with soap, so the water is softened.

> Magnesium ions also cause hardness in water, and these ions are also swapped for sodium ions from the resin.

ion exchange column

calcium ions displace sodium ions from the resin molecules

resin molecules

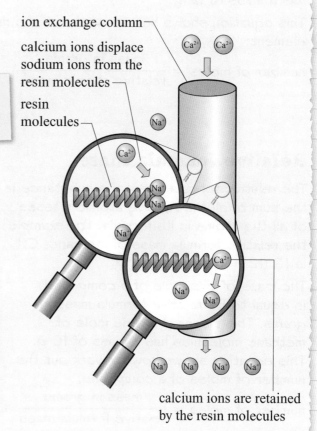

calcium ions are retained by the resin molecules

Now try this

1. target E-C

   (a) Name the substance that causes temporary hardness in water. **(1 mark)**

   (b) Name a substance that causes permanent hardness in water. **(1 mark)**

   (c) Explain why temporary hardness can be removed by boiling. **(2 marks)**

2. target D-C

   (a) Explain why both types of hardness can be removed using an ion exchange resin. **(2 marks)**

   (b) Dishwashing machines contain an ion exchange column. Suggest why salt – sodium chloride – must be added to dishwashing machines every few weeks. **(3 marks)**

Moles and mass

HIGHER This whole page covers Higher material.

The amount of a substance can be measured in grams, numbers of particles, or number of moles of particles.

Moles

Avogadro's number (6.02×10^{23}) is the number of carbon atoms in 12 g of carbon. One mole of any type of particle contains this number of particles, whether they are atoms, ions or molecules.

The mass of one mole (1 mol) of atoms of an element is equal to its relative atomic mass given in grams. For example: 1 mol of hydrogen atoms has a mass of 1 g and 1 mol of carbon atoms has a mass of 12 g.

This equation shows how to work out the number of moles of an element:

$$\text{number of moles} = \frac{\text{mass in grams}}{\text{relative atomic mass}}$$

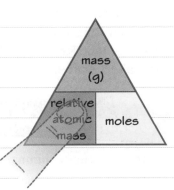

Relative formula mass

The relative formula mass of a substance is the sum of all the relative atomic masses of all the atoms in its formula. For example, the relative formula mass of methane, CH_4, is 16 ($12 + 1 + 1 + 1 + 1$).

The mass of one mole of a compound is equal to its relative formula mass in grams. This means that one mole of methane molecules has a mass of 16 g. This equation shows how to work out the number of moles of a compound:

$$\text{number of moles} = \frac{\text{mass in grams}}{\text{relative formula mass}}$$

Worked example

How many moles of ethane molecules are there in 45 g of ethane, C_2H_6? (Relative atomic mass of carbon = 12, hydrogen = 1)

relative formula mass
$= (2 \times 12) + (6 \times 1) = 30$

number of moles
$= 45 \div 30 = 1.5$ mol

Remember to calculate the relative formula mass first if you have not been given it in the question.

Now try this

1. Calculate the relative formula masses of the following substances. Use these relative atomic masses:
    O = 16, H = 1, C = 12.
    (a) oxygen (O_2) **(1 mark)**
    (b) water (H_2O) **(1 mark)**
    (c) ethanol (C_2H_5OH) **(1 mark)**

2. (a) Calculate the number of moles of carbon atoms in 6 g of carbon.
    (2 marks)
    (b) Calculate the number of moles of hydrogen molecules in 4 g of hydrogen, H_2. **(2 marks)**

Moles in solution

HIGHER This whole page covers Higher material.

The concentration of a solute in a solution can be measured in $g\ dm^{-3}$ or in $mol\ dm^{-3}$. It is possible to convert between the two units.

Moles to mass

You can calculate the mass of a given number of moles of a substance if you know its relative atomic mass, or its relative formula mass:

mass in grams = relative atomic mass × number of moles

mass in grams = relative formula mass × number of moles

Worked example

What is the mass of 0.1 mol of oxygen molecules, O_2? (The relative atomic mass of oxygen is 16.)

Relative formula mass of O_2 = 16 + 16 = 32

Mass of 0.1 mol = 32 × 0.1 = 3.2 g

> Notice that the relative formula mass of oxygen is used here. Although oxygen is an element, it exists as molecules, each consisting of two oxygen atoms.

Solution calculations

The concentration of a solute in a solution can be measured in $mol\ dm^{-3}$ (moles per cubic decimetre).

$$\text{concentration (mol dm}^{-3}) = \frac{\text{moles of solute (mol)}}{\text{volume of solution (dm}^3)}$$

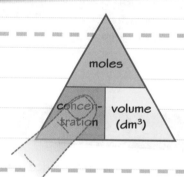

Conversions

You can easily convert between $g\ dm^{-3}$ and $mol\ dm^{-3}$ if you know the relative formula mass of the solute:

- $g\ dm^{-3}$ to $mol\ dm^{-3}$: divide the concentration by the relative formula mass
- $mol\ dm^{-3}$ to $g\ dm^{-3}$: multiply the concentration by the relative formula mass

Worked example

What is the concentration in $g\ dm^{-3}$ of a $0.25\ mol\ dm^{-3}$ solution of sodium hydroxide? The relative formula mass of sodium hydroxide is 40.

concentration
= 0.25 mol dm^{-3} × 40 = 10 g dm^{-3}

Now try this

target **C–A***

Use these relative atomic masses:
H = 1, O = 16, Mg = 24.

1. Calculate the mass of 0.25 mol of magnesium oxide, MgO. **(2 marks)**

2. 200 cm³ of 'Milk of Magnesia' contains 0.04 mol of magnesium hydroxide in solution, $Mg(OH)_2$. Calculate the concentration of magnesium hydroxide in:
   (a) mol dm^{-3} **(2 marks)**
   (b) g dm^{-3}. **(2 marks)**

Preparing soluble salts 1

Soluble salts can be made using an acid and an excess of an insoluble base, such as copper oxide.

Using an insoluble reactant

The diagrams show the three main steps needed to make a soluble salt from an insoluble base.

 Add an excess of insoluble base

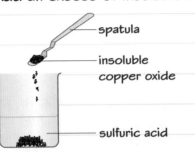
- spatula
- insoluble copper oxide
- sulfuric acid

An excess of the insoluble base has been added when some of it is left over after the reaction stops. Using an excess makes sure that all the acid has reacted.

2 Remove excess insoluble base by filtration

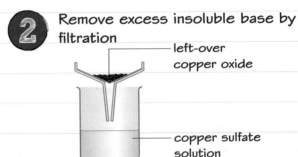
- left-over copper oxide
- copper sulfate solution

Filtration removes the excess insoluble base from the mixture. The salt solution passes through as the filtrate.

3 Evaporate to produce crystals of the salt

- copper sulfate crystals formed by evaporating the solution

Worked example

(a) State the reactants needed to make a sample of magnesium nitrate, $Mg(NO_3)_2$, from an insoluble base.

You would need magnesium oxide and nitric acid.

> Hydrochloric acid makes chlorides, nitric acid makes nitrates, and sulfuric acid makes sulfates.

(b) Write a word equation and a balanced equation for the reaction.

magnesium oxide + nitric acid → magnesium nitrate + water

$$MgO(s) + 2HNO_3(aq) \rightarrow Mg(NO_3)_2 + H_2O(l)$$

> The solution produced only contains the salt and water.

Now try this

 target E-C

1. Zinc chloride is a soluble salt made by reacting zinc oxide with hydrochloric acid.
   (a) Write a word equation for the reaction. **(1 mark)**
   (b) State why an excess of zinc oxide is needed when making zinc chloride. **(1 mark)**

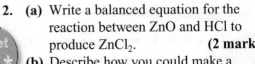 **target C-A*** **HIGHER**

2. **(a)** Write a balanced equation for the reaction between ZnO and HCl to produce $ZnCl_2$. **(2 marks)**
   (b) Describe how you could make a sample of pure, solid zinc chloride. **(3 marks)**

Preparing soluble salts 2

Soluble salts can be made using an acid and an exact amount of a soluble base, such as sodium hydroxide solution.

Using a soluble reactant

The flow chart shows the three main steps needed to make a soluble salt from a soluble base.

| Use an acid–base titration to find the exact volume of the soluble base that reacts with the acid. | → | Mix the acid and soluble base in the correct proportions, producing a solution of the salt and water. | → | Warm the salt solution to evaporate the water – this will leave crystals of the salt behind. |

Neutralisation

Acids release hydrogen ions $H^+(aq)$ when they dissolve in water. Soluble bases (alkalis) release hydroxide ions $OH^-(aq)$ when they dissolve in water.

An acid-base titration involves a neutralisation reaction in which the hydrogen ions from the acid react with the hydroxide ions from the base. This is the ionic equation:

$$H^+(aq) + OH^-(aq) \rightarrow H_2O(l)$$

Worked example

Describe how you would carry out an accurate titration in which the alkali is placed in a conical flask. Name a suitable indicator and describe its colour change.

Use a pipette to transfer a known volume of alkali to a conical flask. Add a few drops of phenolphthalein indicator. Fill the burette with acid and note the reading. Open the tap and add acid to the alkali. Swirl the flask to mix the contents. Near the end, the indicator will start to change from pink to colourless. Adjust the tap to add the alkali drop by drop near the end point. Close the tap at the end point and note the new burette reading. Repeat until you get concordant results.

EXAM ALERT!

Make sure you can describe how to carry out an accurate titration. In a recent exam question on this topic less than half of all students achieved full marks.

Students have struggled with this topic in recent exams - **be prepared!** ResultsPlus

It is good practice only to add the liquid drop by drop near the end point.

The difference between the start and end readings is the volume of acid needed to react with the base without leaving an excess. Concordant results are close to each other or identical.

Now try this

 target E-C

1. (a) Name a suitable indicator for a titration. **(1 mark)**
    (b) State what is meant by concordant results. **(1 mark)**

 target C-A* HIGHER

2. Describe two steps you would take to obtain an accurate result in a titration. **(2 marks)**

3. Write the ionic equation for neutralisation. Include state symbols. **(2 marks)**

Titration calculations

HIGHER This whole page covers Higher material.

Calculating a concentration

In a titration, you will know the concentration and volume of one of the reagents. You will only know the volume of the other reagent – its concentration will have to be calculated using the mean volume from the titration. The worked example below shows you the steps needed to do this.

> A titration should be repeated to identify any anomalous values. Calculate the volume of solution added from the burette by subtracting the start reading from the end reading in each run. Any anomalous volumes should be left out when calculating the mean volume added.

Worked example

25.00 cm^3 of sodium hydroxide solution was pipetted into a conical flask. It was titrated against 0.10 mol dm^{-3} hydrochloric acid. The mean volume of acid needed was 24.00 cm^3.

> Divide by 1000 to convert from cm^3 to dm^3.

(a) Write the balanced equation for the reaction.

HCl + NaOH → NaCl + H$_2$O

(b) Calculate the concentration of sodium hydroxide used in the titration above.

> Notice that you do not need to use any relative atomic masses or relative formula masses in these calculations.

Volume of HCl = 24.00 cm^3 ÷ 1000 = 0.024 dm^3

Number of moles of HCl = concentration × volume

= 0.10 mol dm^{-3} × 0.024 dm^3 = 0.0024 mol

From the equation, 1 mol of HCl reacts with 1 mol of NaOH, so there will be 0.0024 mol of NaOH

Volume of NaOH = 25.00 cm^3 ÷ 1000 = 0.025 dm^3

Concentration of NaOH = number of moles ÷ volume

= 0.0024 mol ÷ 0.025 dm^3 = 0.096 mol dm^{-3}

Now try this

1. 25.00 cm^3 of potassium hydroxide, KOH, solution was pipetted into a conical flask. It was titrated against 0.20 mol dm^{-3} nitric acid, HNO$_3$.

    (a) A group of students carried out the experiment three times and the volume of acid used was 25.5cm^3, 29.0 cm^3 and 27.5 cm^3. Calculate the mean volume of the acid used. **(2 marks)**

    (b) With another group of students the mean volume of the acid used was 28.00 cm^3. Calculate the concentration of potassium hydroxide solution.

    (3 marks)

EXAM ALERT!

A titration calculation like this one is usually worth three marks in the examination. In a recent examination, less than one in ten of students gained full marks and over half only gained one mark. Remember to show your working out.

Students have struggled with this topic in recent exams - **be prepared!**   Results Plus

More calculations from equations

HIGHER This whole page covers Higher material.

Calculating a volume

You can use mole calculations to predict the volume of one reagent that will neutralise a measured volume of another reagent. To do this, you need to know the concentrations of both reactants.

Worked example

(a) Write the balanced equation for the reaction between sulfuric acid and sodium hydroxide.

$$H_2SO_4 + 2NaOH \rightarrow Na_2SO_4 + 2H_2O$$

> Notice that 1 mol of H_2SO_4 reacts with 2 mol of NaOH. This is different than the situation when hydrochloric acid is used, when 1 mol of HCl reacts with just 1 mol of NaOH:
>
> $$HCl + NaOH \rightarrow NaCl + H_2O$$

(b) What volume of 1.0 mol dm^{-3} sulfuric acid will be needed to neutralise 25.00 cm^3 of 0.8 mol dm^{-3} sodium hydroxide solution?

Volume of NaOH = 25.00 cm^3 ÷ 1000 = 0.025 dm^3

> Divide by 1000 to convert from cm^3 to dm^3.

Number of moles of NaOH = concentration × volume

$\qquad\qquad$ = 0.8 mol dm^{-3} × 0.025 dm^3 = 0.02 mol

From the equation, 1 mol of H_2SO_4 reacts with 2 mol of NaOH, so there will be 0.01 mol of H_2SO_4

> The 'mole ratio' between sulfuric acid and sodium hydroxide solution is 1:2 – this is why the number of moles of sulfuric acid is half the number of moles of sodium hydroxide.

Volume of H_2SO_4 = number of moles ÷ concentration

$\qquad\qquad$ = 0.01 mol ÷ 1.0 mol dm^{-3} = 0.01 dm^3 (or 10 cm^3)

> Multiply by 1000 to convert from dm^3 to cm^3.

Now try this

1. Calculate the volume of 0.5 mol dm^{-3} hydrochloric acid needed to neutralise 25.00 cm^3 of 0.20 mol dm^{-3} sodium hydroxide solution. **(3 marks)**

2. Calculate the volume of 0.10 mol dm^{-3} sodium hydroxide solution needed to neutralise 20.00 cm^3 of 0.25 mol dm^{-3} hydrochloric acid. **(3 marks)**

3. Calculate the volume of 0.25 mol dm^{-3} sulfuric acid needed to neutralise 20.00 cm^3 of 0.10 mol dm^{-3} sodium hydroxide solution. **(3 marks)**

Chemistry extended writing 1

To answer an extended writing question successfuly you need to:
- ✓ use your scientific knowledge to answer the question
- ✓ organise your answer so that it is logical and well ordered
- ✓ use full sentences in your writing and make sure that your spelling, punctuation and grammar are correct.

Worked example

Ammonium bromide, NH_4Br, is a white solid.

Describe chemical tests that you could carry on an unknown solid to identify if it is ammonium bromide. You should include balanced chemical equations for any tests that you describe.   **(6 marks)**

Sample answer 1

You can do a flame test for the ammonium ion and the flame goes yellow. To test for bromide ions, you add silver nitrate. This makes a sort of creamy-white precipitate of silver bromide.

This is a basic answer. The flame test is not correct – ammonium ions do not give a flame colour. The test for the bromide ion is correct, although it does not give the other reagent added. However, it does identify the substance that makes the cream precipitate.

Sample answer 2

Ammonium ion: add sodium hydroxide solution. This makes ammonia gas, which has a nasty smell. It's also alkaline.

Bromide ion: add nitric acid and then silver nitrate solution. This makes a creamy precipitate. The equation is NH_4Br (aq) + $AgNO_3$ (aq) → AgBr (s) + NH_4NO_3 (aq)

This is a good answer. The description of the bromide ion test is very good: the chemical substances suggested for the test are correct and 'creamy' is OK although 'cream' is more usual. The equation is also correct, including the state symbols. The test for the ammonium ion is mostly correct, but there are some important details missing. The solution usually needs warming, and there should be a test given for ammonia gas (using moist red litmus paper). These details would make the answer excellent – if you added the equation for the reaction of ammonium bromide with sodium hydroxide to make ammonia gas, the examiner would be very impressed indeed!

Now try this

1. A chemist wants to make a sample of the soluble salt potassium chloride. He has been given a solution of potassium hydroxide and some hydrochloric acid.

    Describe how he would make pure, dry crystals of potassium chloride.   **(6 marks)**

Remember that the method you need here is titration. You need to say how this method works. Remember that the final crystals made need to be dry and pure.

Chemistry extended writing 2

Worked example

Explain why different methods are needed to treat hardness in different types of hard water. **(6 marks)**

Sample answer 1

There are two types of hard water – temporary hard water and permanent hard water. Both types of water contain dissolved calcium or magnesium ions. This is what makes the water hard. Hard water does not lather easily with soap and makes scum. If hard water is distilled, it becomes softer. The other method that can be used is an ion exchange resin. This removes the calcium ions so that the water becomes soft.

This is a good answer. Although it is useful to say what hard water is, this answer contains a little too much irrelevant information on the properties of hard water. (You do not lose marks for putting in irrelevant information, but you are wasting examination time by doing this!) Although the information about distillation is true, this is not a usual method of water softening. The description of ion exchange resin is good, although more detail could be given. The answer does not compare the different methods that can be used to soften temporary hard water.

Sample answer 2

Temporary hard water is called temporary because the hardness is easy to remove. This is done by boiling the water. Temporary hard water contains calcium hydrogencarbonate. When it is heated, the hydrocarbonate decomposes to make calcium carbonate, which appears as limescale. The calcium ions are removed from the water and it becomes soft. Boiling only works for temporary hard water. Permanent hard water contains different dissolved calcium compounds. To remove the hardness from permanent hard water, you need an ion exchange resin. The resin contains sodium ions. As the hard water travels through the resin, sodium ions in the resin swap with calcium ions in the water, so the water becomes soft. Ion exchange resins also work on temporary hard water.

This is an excellent answer. There is a good description of how boiling removes temporary hardness. The description of the way an ion exchange resin works is also very good and clear. Although the question does not ask for any equations, you could choose to add a word or symbol equation showing the decomposition of calcium hydrogencarbonate to calcium carbonate.

Now try this

1. A student has been asked to make crystals of the soluble salt, nickel sulfate, using sulfuric acid and the insoluble base, nickel carbonate. Describe the method she should use to make a sample of the salt.
   (6 marks)

Electrolysis

Ionic substances can be broken down using electricity, forming useful elements or compounds. This process is called electrolysis.

Electrolytes

Worked example

Explain why sodium chloride will conduct electricity when it is molten or in solution, but it will not conduct electricity when it is solid.

The ions in sodium chloride are free to move when it is melted to form a liquid, or when it is dissolved in water. This allows it to conduct electricity. Solid sodium chloride cannot conduct electricity because its ions are not free to move around.

A substance that contains free ions, letting it conduct electricity, is called an electrolyte. This could have been mentioned in the answer.

Remember that the ions in a solid can move a little by vibrating, but they cannot move from place to place.

Electrolysis

Electrolysis needs a direct current (d.c.). Electrodes are made from graphite or unreactive metals such as copper or platinum. During electrolysis:

- Positive ions (cations) are attracted to the negative electrode (cathode). They gain electrons there and so are reduced.

Remember that 'cat' ions are 'puss-itive'.

- Negative ions (anions) are attracted to the positive electrode (anode). They lose electrons there and so are oxidised.

Remember 'OIL-RIG' – Oxidation Is Loss of electrons, Reduction Is Gain of electrons.

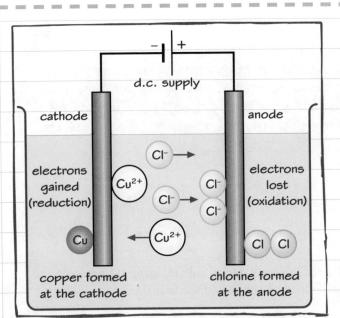

Electrolysis of aqueous copper chloride

Now try this

 target E-C

1. (a) State what is meant by an electrolyte. **(1 mark)**

   (b) State which electrode cations move towards. **(1 mark)**

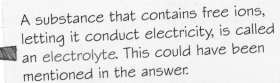 target D-B

2. Explain why a solution of copper chloride is an electrolyte but solid copper chloride is not. **(2 marks)**

 target C-A

3. Describe the overall movement of the ions in molten sodium chloride during electrolysis. **(2 marks)**

HIGHER

Making and using sodium

Sodium is a useful metal. It is manufactured by the electrolysis of molten sodium chloride.

Electrolysis of molten sodium chloride

This shows a simple laboratory experiment. You do not need to know any details of industrial electrolytic cells for the examination.

Molten sodium chloride contains sodium ions (Na^+) and chloride ions (Cl^-).

EXAM ALERT!

Be careful if you are asked to say what you would see during electrolysis. For example, you would not see chloride ions moving to the anode, but you would see bubbles of gas forming there. In a recent examination, only around one in five of students gained full marks for correctly stating what they would see, rather than describing the processes or just repeating part of the question.

Students have struggled with this topic in recent exams - **be prepared!**

Results**Plus**

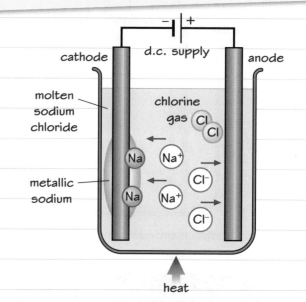

cathode   d.c. supply   anode

molten sodium chloride

chlorine gas Cl Cl

Na Na^+

metallic sodium

Na Na^+ Cl^-

Cl^-

heat

Uses of sodium

Sodium is used in street lamps. A bright yellow light is given out when an electric current is passed through sodium vapour in the lamp.

Liquid sodium has a high 'heat capacity' (it takes a lot of heat energy to raise its temperature). This makes it useful as a coolant in some nuclear power stations.

Half equations

Worked example

 HIGHER

Write balanced half equations for the reactions at the cathode and anode during the electrolysis of molten potassium chloride. For each one, state whether it represents oxidation or reduction.

At the cathode:
$K^+(l) + e^- \rightarrow K(l)$ (reduction)

At the anode:
$2Cl^-(l) \rightarrow Cl_2(g) + 2e^-$ (oxidation)

Now try this

target **E-C**

1. Explain one use of sodium.   **(2 marks)**

2. Describe what you would see at the anode during the electrolysis of molten sodium chloride.   **(1 mark)**

target **C-A*** HIGHER

3. Sodium is manufactured by the electrolysis of molten sodium chloride.
   (a) Write half equations for the reactions that happen at each electrode.   **(4 marks)**
   (b) For each of the half equations in part (a), explain whether it represents reduction or oxidation.   **(2 marks)**

Electrolysis of salt water

The electrolysis of aqueous sodium chloride provides three useful industrial products: hydrogen, chlorine and sodium hydroxide solution.

Electrolysis of sodium chloride solution

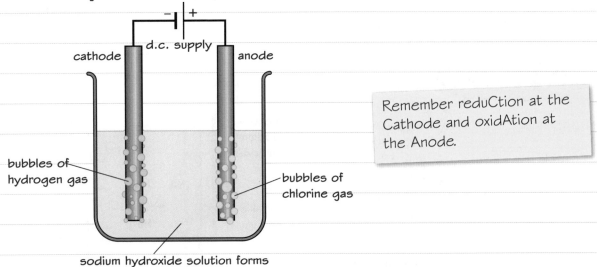

cathode   d.c. supply   anode

bubbles of hydrogen gas

bubbles of chlorine gas

sodium hydroxide solution forms

> Remember reduCtion at the Cathode and oxidAtion at the Anode.

Worked example   HIGHER

Potassium chloride behaves in a similar way to sodium chloride during electrolysis.

(a) Identify the ions present in a solution of potassium chloride, and explain where they come from.

Potassium ions (K^+) and chloride ions (Cl^-) from the dissolved potassium chloride. Hydrogen ions (H^+) and hydroxide ions (OH^-) from the water in the solution.

(b) Use half equations to describe the reactions at each electrode.

At the cathode: $2H^+(aq) + 2e^- \rightarrow H_2(g)$
At the anode: $2Cl^-(aq) \rightarrow Cl_2(g) + 2e^-$

(c) Write an ionic equation to show why potassium hydroxide solution forms.

In the electrolyte: $K^+(aq) + OH^-(aq) \rightarrow KOH(aq)$

> A small number of water molecules ionise to form $H^+(aq)$ ions and $OH^-(aq)$ ions. These are present in all aqueous solutions (mixtures made by dissolving substances in water). They also move towards the electrodes during electrolysis.

> It could have been explained that this is reduction because the hydrogen ions gain electrons.

> It could have been explained that this is oxidation because the chloride ions lose electrons.

Now try this

target E-C

1. **(a)** Name the gas formed at each electrode during the electrolysis of sodium chloride solution. **(2 marks)**
   (b) State why sodium chloride solution contains hydrogen ions and hydroxide ions. **(1 mark)**

target C-A*
HIGHER

2. The electrolysis of aqueous sodium chloride produces three useful products.
   (a) Give the formulae of the ions present in aqueous sodium chloride. **(2 marks)**
   (b) Write a half equation for the reaction that happens at each electrode. **(4 marks)**
   (c) Explain why a solution of sodium hydroxide forms. **(2 marks)**

More electrolysis

Purifying copper

Copper is purified or refined industrially using electrolysis.

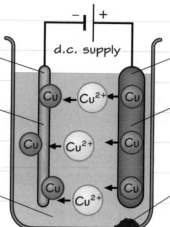

pure copper cathode

d.c. supply

impure copper anode

copper ions move to the copper electrode, gain electrons and are discharged as pure copper

ions are replaced by copper ions from the impure copper anode

copper sulfate solution

impurities form a 'sludge' below the anode – this contains metals such as silver, gold and platinum

Predicting the products of electrolysis

It is usually easy to predict the products of the electrolysis of a molten electrolyte. For example, molten lead bromide produces lead and bromine. When the electrolyte is a solution, hydrogen ions and hydroxide ions from the water may be discharged instead. For example, copper sulfate solution produces copper at the cathode and oxygen at the anode, but sodium sulfate solution produces hydrogen at the cathode and oxygen at the anode.

Hydrogen ions are discharged unless the metal is less reactive than hydrogen.

Hydroxide ions are discharged (producing oxygen) unless chloride, bromide or iodide ions are present.

Electroplating

Worked example

(a) Explain why electroplating is carried out.

Electroplating improves the appearance of metal objects and their resistance to corrosion. Jewellery may be electroplated with silver or gold. Galvanised steel is steel coated with a thin layer of zinc to improve its resistance to rusting.

(b) Describe how electroplating is carried out.

The cathode is the object to be electroplated. The anode is the plating metal. The electrolyte contains ions of the plating metal. During electroplating, ions from the electrolyte move to the object and are discharged as metal atoms. They are replaced by ions leaving the anode.

Now try this

target
E–C

1. **(a)** Describe what you would see at each electrode during the purification of copper by electrolysis. **(2 marks)**
   (b) A steel spoon is to be electroplated with silver. State what the anode and cathode should be made from. **(2 marks)**

target
C–A*

HIGHER

2. Copper is purified by electrolysis.
   (a) Explain why the mass of the impure copper electrode decreases. **(2 marks)**
   (b) Explain why the electrolyte is copper sulfate solution. **(2 marks)**
   (c) Suggest why the anode 'sludge' helps to reduce the overall cost of purifying copper. **(2 marks)**

Gas calculations 1

HIGHER This whole page covers Higher material.

Molar volume

Avogadro's Law means that equal volumes of gases contain an equal number of particles, if they are at the same temperature and pressure.

This means that, at a given temperature and pressure, one mole of any gas will occupy the same volume. At room temperature and atmospheric pressure, one mole of any gas occupies 24 dm³. This volume is called the molar volume of the gas.

Calculating volumes

The volume of a gas can be calculated using the molar volume:

volume = number of moles × molar volume

Worked example

What is the volume of 0.5 mol of nitrogen at room temperature and atmospheric pressure?

volume = number of moles × molar volume

= 0.5 × 24 dm³ = 12 dm³

Calculating moles

The number of moles of a gas can be calculated using the molar volume:

$$\text{number of moles} = \frac{\text{volume}}{\text{molar volume}}$$

Worked example

How many moles of carbon dioxide occupy 240 cm³ at room temperature and atmospheric pressure? (molar volume = 24 000 cm³)

number of moles = volume ÷ molar volume

= 240 ÷ 24 000

= 0.01 mol

EXAM ALERT!

You will be given the molar volume in the examination, but make sure you know how to use it. In a recent examination less than half the candidates could calculate the number of moles of carbon dioxide in 120 cm³. Many used the relative formula mass, which is not needed.

Students have struggled with this topic in recent exams - **be prepared!**   ResultsPlus

Now try this

1. Explain which gas contains the most molecules at room temperature and atmospheric pressure, 1 mol of carbon dioxide (relative formula mass = 44) or 1 mol of nitrogen (relative formula mass = 28). **(2 marks)**

target C-B

2. Calculate the volume of 0.1 mol of hydrogen at room temperature and atmospheric pressure (1 mol occupies 24 dm³). **(1 mark)**

target B-A*

3. Calculate the number of moles of hydrogen in 120 cm³ at room temperature and atmospheric pressure (1 mol occupies 24 000 cm³). **(1 mark)**

Gas calculations 2

HIGHER This whole page covers Higher material.

Reacting volumes

Worked example

Calculate the maximum volume of ammonia, NH_3, that can be made from 30 cm³ of hydrogen, H_2.

$$N_2(g) + 3H_2(g) \rightarrow 2NH_3(g)$$

The ratio of $NH_3:H_2$ is 2:3, so 30 cm³ × $\frac{2}{3}$ = 20 cm³ of ammonia can be made.

EXAM ALERT!

Use the balancing numbers in the chemical equation to help you work out the volumes of the gases in the reaction. In a recent examination, only a fifth of candidates used them correctly.

Students have struggled with this topic in recent exams - **be prepared!**   Results Plus

Solids and gases

Worked example

Sulfur burns in oxygen to produce sulfur dioxide:

$$S(s) + O_2(g) \rightarrow SO_2(g)$$

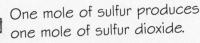 One mole of sulfur produces one mole of sulfur dioxide.

Calculate the maximum volume of sulfur dioxide (at room temperature and atmospheric pressure) that can be produced from 16 g of sulfur (relative atomic mass of S is 32, molar volume is 24 dm³).

moles of sulfur = mass ÷ relative atomic mass
= 16 ÷ 32 = 0.5 mol

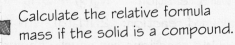 Calculate the relative formula mass if the solid is a compound.

volume of sulfur dioxide
= number of moles × molar volume
= 0.5 mol × 24 dm³ = 12 dm³

Now try this

target B-A*

1. Carbon dioxide breathed out by astronauts is removed in spacecraft using containers of lithium hydroxide, LiOH:

$$2LiOH(s) + CO_2(g) \rightarrow Li_2CO_3(s) + H_2O(g)$$

(a) Calculate the number of moles of carbon dioxide in 540 dm³ of carbon dioxide at room temperature and pressure (molar volume = 24 dm³ at room temperature and pressure).
(1 mark)

(b) Calculate the number of moles of lithium hydroxide needed to absorb this volume of carbon dioxide.
(1 mark)

Fertilisers

Nitrogenous fertilisers

Fertilisers replace the soil minerals used by plants as they grow. Fertilisers promote plant growth, increasing crop yields for farmers. Nitrogenous fertilisers contain nitrogen compounds.

Making fertilisers

Nitrogenous fertilisers are made from ammonia (NH_3). Ammonia is made from nitrogen and hydrogen in the Haber process (see page 56):

- nitrogen is extracted from the air
- hydrogen is made from natural gas – this is mostly methane (CH_4).

Worked example

Describe the consequences for rivers and lakes of using too much nitrogenous fertiliser.

Excess fertiliser can be washed out of the soil and into rivers and lakes when it rains. The extra minerals cause water plants to grow quickly. They cover the surface and stop light getting in. Plants underneath die and are decomposed by bacteria. These use up the oxygen in the water, causing fish to die.

Reversible reactions

Some chemical reactions are reversible: the reaction can go in both directions. For the Haber process:

- forward reaction: $N_2(g) + 3H_2 \rightarrow 2NH_3(g)$
- backward reaction: $2NH_3(g) \rightarrow N_2(g) + 3H_2(g)$

Reversible reactions are usually shown as a single equation with the reversible symbol instead of an arrow:

nitrogen + hydrogen $\rightleftharpoons$ ammonia

$$N_2(g) + 3H_2(g) \rightleftharpoons 2NH_3(g)$$

The reaction from left to right is called the forward reaction, and the reaction from right to left is called the backward reaction.

Now try this

1. State two raw materials for making ammonia by the Haber process. **(2 marks)**

2. Describe what happens in the backward reaction in the Haber process. **(2 marks)**

3. Explain, using the Haber process as an example, what a reversible reaction is. **(2 marks)**

Equilibrium

HIGHER This whole page covers Higher material.

Dynamic equilibrium

A reversible reaction may reach equilibrium if it happens in a closed container. For example, in the Haber process nitrogen and hydrogen react to make ammonia:

nitrogen + hydrogen $\rightleftharpoons$ ammonia

At equilibrium, the rate of the forward reaction and the rate of the backward reaction are the same. The concentrations of all the substances involved stay constant. It is called a dynamic equilibrium because both reactions are still happening.

Forward reaction: the concentration of nitrogen and hydrogen decrease as they are used up to make ammonia. This means that the rate of the forward reaction decreases.

rate of forward reaction = rate of backward reaction at equilibrium

Backward reaction: the concentration of ammonia increases so the rate of the backwards reaction increases.

(graph: Rate vs Time)

Position of equilibrium

The concentrations of all substances at equilibrium do not have to be the same as each other. If the concentrations of the substances on the right of the equation are greater than the concentrations of the substances on the left, we say that the position of equilibrium is to the right.

If a reversible reaction involves gases and the pressure is increased, the position of equilibrium moves in the direction of the fewest molecules of gas.

If the temperature is increased the position of the equilibrium moves in the direction of the endothermic change.

Worked example

The forward reaction is exothermic when sulfur trioxide is produced from sulfur dioxide and oxygen. What happens to the yield of sulfur trioxide if the temperature is increased?

If the forward reaction is exothermic, the backward reaction must be endothermic. When the temperature is increased, the position of equilibrium will move in the endothermic direction. This will decrease the yield of sulfur trioxide.

If the forward reaction is endothermic instead, the backward reaction will be exothermic.

Now try this

1. Hydrogen reacts with iodine vapour to form hydrogen iodide:

$$H_2(g) + I_2(g) \rightleftharpoons 2HI(g)$$

target B-A*

Explain what change, if any, will happen to the position of equilibrium in this reaction if the pressure is increased. **(2 marks)**

2. When cooled, NO_2 gas forms N_2O_4 gas. The reaction reaches equilibrium in a sealed container:

$$2NO_2(g) \rightleftharpoons N_2O_4(g)$$

(a) Explain what happens to the equilibrium yield of NO_2 if the pressure is increased. **(3 marks)**

(b) Explain whether the forward reaction is exothermic or endothermic. **(2 marks)**

The Haber process

HIGHER This whole page covers Higher material.

Catalysts

A catalyst is a substance that speeds up the rate of a reaction without being used up. In a reversible reaction, a catalyst increases the rate of both the forward reaction and the backward reaction by the same amount. This means that a catalyst does not change the position of equilibrium, but it does reduce the time needed to reach equilibrium. Catalysts are important for reducing costs in industrial processes.

The Haber process

The Haber process is an industrial process for manufacturing ammonia:

$$N_2(g) + 3H_2(g) \rightleftharpoons 2NH_3(g)$$

The conditions needed for the Haber process are usually: an iron catalyst, a high pressure (about 200 times atmospheric pressure) and a temperature of about 450°C.

Worked example

(a) Explain why a high pressure is needed in the Haber process.

There are four molecules of gas on the left-hand side of the equation, but only two molecules on the right-hand side. If the pressure is increased, the position of equilibrium moves to the right, increasing the yield of ammonia.

(b) Explain why pressures above 200 atmospheres are not used.

Very high pressures would need stronger and more expensive equipment.

> The answer links the use of high pressure to the high yield of ammonia using the idea of how to change the position of equilibrium.

The forward reaction in the Haber process is exothermic. You would expect to use a low temperature because the position of equilibrium would move to the right. However, if the temperature were too low, the rate of reaction would be too low. So 450°C is a compromise temperature – low enough to get an acceptable yield of ammonia but high enough to get it in an acceptable time.

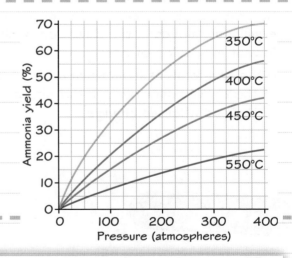

Now try this

target C-B

1. Explain why catalysts are important in industrial chemical processes.
   (2 marks)

2. The conditions used in the Haber process are usually 200 atmospheres of pressure and a temperature of 450°C.

   (a) Use the graph to state the yield of ammonia under these conditions.
   (1 mark)

   (b) (i) State an advantage and a disadvantage of using a pressure higher than 200 atmospheres.
   (2 marks)

   (ii) State an advantage and a disadvantage of using a lower temperature than 450°C.
   (2 marks)

Chemistry extended writing 3

Worked example   HIGHER

A student is investigating the effect of electrolysis on two solutions – copper sulfate solution and potassium bromide solution. The table shows the observations he makes.

Solution	Negative electrode	Positive electrode
copper sulfate	pinky-brown solid forms on electrode	bubbles of gas
potassium chloride	bubbles of gas	bubbles of gas and strong smell of bleach

Explain these observations. You should give the tests that the student could use carry out to identify the products at the electrodes. You should also include balanced equations for electrode reactions.   **(6 marks)**

Sample answer 1

Copper sulfate solution makes copper at the negative electrode and sulfur dioxide at the positive electrode. You can test for sulfur dioxide because it is acidic. The potassium chloride makes hydrogen at the negative electrode. The smell at the positive electrode is because of chloride gas being made.

This is a basic answer. It correctly identifies both the products at the negative electrode, although it could be improved by giving equations for their formation, or a test for hydrogen. However, the products at the positive electrodes are not correct – both show common errors. Although there are sulfate ions present in copper sulfate, they stay in solution and the electrode product is oxygen. Lastly, remember that chloriDe is the name of the ion – the element formed in electrolysis is chloriNe.

Sample answer 2

Copper sulfate: copper is formed at the negative electrode and oxygen is formed at the positive electrode. You can test for oxygen, as it relights a glowing splint. The equation for the formation of copper is Cu^{2+} (aq) $+ 2e^- \rightarrow Cu$ (s). The oxygen comes from the water.

Potassium chloride: hydrogen is produced at the negative electrode – it burns with a squeaky pop. The equation is $2H^+$ (aq) $+ 2e^- \rightarrow H_2$ (g). At the positive electrode, the gas and smell are caused by chlorine being made. This equation is $2Cl^-$ (aq) $\rightarrow Cl_2$ (aq) $+ 2e^-$. The test for chlorine is to use damp litmus paper, but the bleachy smell is characteristic.

This is an excellent answer. It does miss out the equation for the formation of water at the positive electrode for copper sulfate – but this is a very hard equation to remember. As the answer says, the smell is pretty distinctive for chlorine, but the answer could add that the litmus paper would be bleached white. No test is needed for copper, as the colour is so distinctive – and there is no test for copper metal on the specification!

Now try this   HIGHER

1. Explain why solid sodium chloride, molten sodium chloride and sodium chloride solution behave differently when they are each placed in an electrolysis cell. Your answer should include balanced equations to illustrate what is happening at the electrodes.   **(6 marks)**

Fermentation and alcohol

Ethanol is the alcohol in beer, wine and other alcoholic drinks. Different drinks contain different amounts of alcohol. For example, beer is usually 4–6% and vodka 40% ethanol.

Fermentation

Ethanol (C_2H_5OH) is produced from carbohydrates by a process called fermentation. Carbon dioxide is also produced in this reaction. The carbohydrates can be sugars from fruit, such as grapes, or from the breakdown of starch from wheat or barley. Yeast is a fungus. It provides enzymes needed for fermentation to happen.

$$\text{sugar} \rightarrow \text{ethanol} + \text{carbon dioxide}$$
$$C_6H_{12}O_6(aq) \rightarrow 2C_2H_5OH(aq) + 2CO_2(g)$$

Worked example

Explain why the fermentation mixture must be kept warm and under anaerobic conditions.

The reaction is too slow at low temperatures and the yeast enzymes do not work at high temperatures. Fermentation is a type of anaerobic respiration. If oxygen is present, aerobic respiration happens instead, producing carbon dioxide and water.

Remember that the enzymes the yeast contains do not work at high temperatures because they are denatured. The optimum temperature for fermentation is around 35°C.

Fractional distillation

Fractional distillation is needed to obtain more concentrated solutions of ethanol.

Effects of alcohol

Alcoholic drinks have harmful effects on the body, including increased reaction times, loss of coordination and vomiting. Long-term excessive drinking causes liver cirrhosis and can damage the heart.

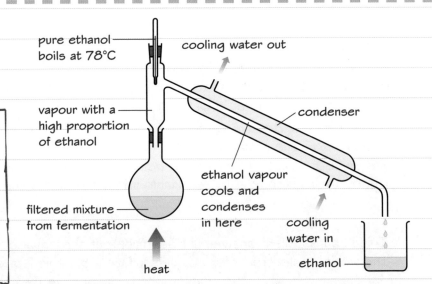

pure ethanol boils at 78°C

cooling water out

vapour with a high proportion of ethanol

condenser

filtered mixture from fermentation

ethanol vapour cools and condenses in here

cooling water in

heat

ethanol

Now try this

target D-B

1. (a) Explain how a concentrated solution of ethanol may be obtained following fermentation. **(2 marks)**
   (b) Explain why the process in part **(a)** is useful to the drinks industry. **(2 marks)**

target C-A
HIGHER

2. Suggest why politicians and doctors may want to impose a minimum price per unit of alcohol. **(2 marks)**

Ethanol production

HIGHER This whole page covers Higher material.

Making ethanol from ethene

Ethanol is not only manufactured by fermentation. It can also be manufactured by the reaction of ethene with steam in the presence of a catalyst. This is a hydration reaction (water is added). The ethene needed is made by cracking crude oil fractions.

Making ethene from ethanol

Ethene can be made by heating ethanol to high temperatures in the presence of a catalyst. This is an example of a dehydration reaction.

Choice of method

The table summarises two factors involved in choosing whether to manufacture ethanol by fermentation or by reacting ethene with steam.

Factor	Fermentation of carbohydrates	Reaction of ethene with steam
source of raw material	plants such as sugar cane or sugar beet	crude oil
quality of final product	ethanol needs separating from the reaction mixture by fractional distillation	pure ethanol

Worked example

Brazil has a few small oil fields and a lot of sugar cane. The country produces large amounts of ethanol by fermentation. This is mixed with petrol to make a fuel called gasohol. Suggest why Brazil makes its ethanol by fermentation rather than by the hydration method.

Sugar from sugar cane can be used as a raw material for making ethanol by fermentation. The hydration method uses ethene, which comes from cracking crude oil fractions. However, fermentation is a better choice in this case because Brazil has a lot of sugar cane but not a lot of oil.

Now try this

1. Describe how ethene can be produced from ethanol. Include a balanced equation in your answer. **(3 marks)**

2. In the UK, ethanol for fuel can be manufactured using sugars from sugar beet or using crude oil. Compare the advantages and disadvantages of each method. **(4 marks)**

Homologous series

An homologous series is a series of compounds that:

- have the same general formula
- show a gradual trend in physical properties (for example, their boiling points increase as the number of carbon atoms in each molecule increases)
- have similar chemical properties. For example they are all flammable.

The alkanes and alkenes belong to two different homologous series. Alkenes can decolourise orange–brown bromine water but alkanes and alcohols cannot do this.

> Make sure your handwriting clearly distinguishes between the **a** in alk**a**nes and the **e** in alk**e**nes.

 Alkanes

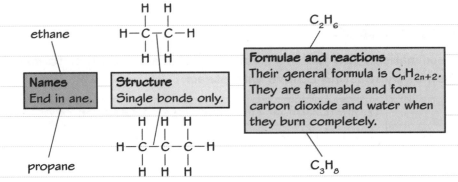

ethane C_2H_6

Names End in ane.

Structure Single bonds only.

Formulae and reactions Their general formula is C_nH_{2n+2}. They are flammable and form carbon dioxide and water when they burn completely.

propane C_3H_8

 Alkenes

> Methane (CH_4) is the simplest alkane. 'Methene' does not exist as it would only have one carbon atom, which could not form a double bond with itself.

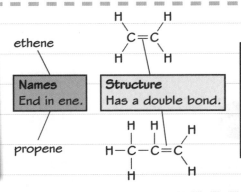

ethene C_2H_4

Names End in ene.

Structure Has a double bond.

Formulae and reactions Their general formula is C_nH_{2n}. They contain carbon–carbon double bonds, which allow them to react with substances such as steam and bromine. They are flammable.

propene C_3H_6

 Alcohols   HIGHER

> Remember:
> meth – 1 carbon atom
> eth – 2 carbons
> prop – 3 carbons
> but – 4 carbons

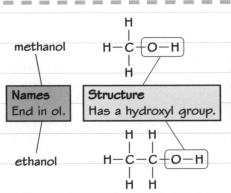

methanol CH_3OH

Names End in ol.

Structure Has a hydroxyl group.

Formulae and reactions The general formula is $C_nH_{2n+1}OH$ and they burn with a cleaner blue flame than the alkanes and alkenes.

ethanol C_2H_5OH

Now try this

 target D-B

1. State two features of a homologous series. **(2 marks)**

2. Butane has four carbon atoms. Give its formula and structure. **(2 marks)**

 target C-A   HIGHER

3. Methanol boils at 65°C and ethanol boils at 78°C. Suggest the boiling point of propanol and give a reason for your answer. **(2 marks)**

target C-A*   HIGHER

4. Describe three differences between alkanes and alkenes. **(3 marks)**

Ethanoic acid

Vinegar

Ethanol can be oxidised to form ethanoic acid. This reaction can happen in open bottles of wine. It is also used in the manufacture of vinegar. Vinegar contains dilute ethanoic acid. It is used as a flavouring and a preservative because bacteria cannot survive in the acidic environment.

Reactions of ethanoic acid

Ethanoic acid has properties typical of acids. For example, it reacts with bases and carbonates to form salts called ethanoates:

sodium hydroxide + ethanoic acid → sodium ethanoate + water

calcium carbonate + ethanoic acid → calcium ethanoate + water + carbon dioxide

Worked example

(a) Explain what colour you would you see when a few drops of universal indicator are added to ethanoic acid solution.

An orange colour because it is an acid.

(b) Magnesium reacts with ethanoic acid to produce a gas and a salt. Give the name of the gas.

Hydrogen.

EXAM ALERT!

In a recent exam, around a third of students could not correctly name the gas produced. Remember that any metal reacting with an acid (or with water) will produce hydrogen.

Students have struggled with this topic in recent exams - **be prepared!** ResultsPlus

Structure of carboxylic acids   HIGHER

Ethanoic acid is a carboxylic acid. Like the alcohols, the carboxylic acids form a homologous series. They contain a carboxyl group (–COOH) and their general formula is $C_nH_{2n+1}COOH$.

Name of alcohol	Number of carbon atoms	Formula
methanoic acid	1	HCOOH
ethanoic acid	2	CH_3COOH
propanoic acid	3	C_2H_5COOH

Now try this

1. Give the name of the type of reaction that produces ethanoic acid from ethanol. **(1 mark)**

2. State two food uses of vinegar. **(2 marks)**

3. Describe two ways in which ethanoic acid reacts like a typical acid. **(2 marks)**

4. (a) Ethanol is C_2H_5OH and ethanoic acid is CH_3COOH. Describe three differences between their structures. **(3 marks)**

(b) The formula for propanoic acid is C_2H_5COOH. Suggest the formula for butanoic acid, which has four carbon atoms. **(1 mark)**

Esters

Uses of esters

The reaction between an alcohol and a carboxylic acid produces an ester and water. For example, when they are warmed in the presence of a sulfuric acid catalyst, ethanol and ethanoic acid react together to form ethyl ethanoate and water. Esters have pleasant, often fruity smells. For example, pentyl ethanoate smells of pear drops.

Worked example

Explain two uses of esters.

Esters are used in perfumes and as food flavourings because they have pleasant smells.

Polyesters

Polyesters are polymers made from two types of monomer. One type of monomer has a carboxyl group at each end and the other has a hydroxyl group at each end. The two types of monomer react together, making polymer molecules containing many ester bonds.

Polyesters can be made into long, thin fibres. These can then be woven together to make fabrics. Polyesters are also used to make drinks bottles. These can be recycled to make fleece, which is used to make clothing.

Making ethyl ethanoate

Ethyl ethanoate is made from ethanoic acid and ethanol:

$$\text{ethanoic acid} \quad + \quad \text{ethanol} \quad \rightarrow \quad \text{ethyl ethanoate} \quad + \quad \text{water}$$

HIGHER $CH_3COOH(aq) + C_2H_5OH(aq) \rightarrow CH_3COOC_2H_5(aq) + H_2O(l)$

ethanoic acid + ethanol

↓

ethyl ethanoate + water

Now try this

1. (a) State two uses of esters. **(2 marks)**

   (b) State the products of the reaction between ethanol and ethanoic acid. **(2 marks)**

2. Explain how polyester drinks bottles may be recycled. **(2 marks)**

3. Write a balanced equation for the formation of ethyl ethanoate, $CH_3COOC_2H_5$, from a carboxylic acid and an alcohol. **(2 marks)**

HIGHER

Fats, oils and soap

Making soap

Oils and fats are esters. Soap is made by boiling oils or fats with a concentrated alkali solution. The esters break down to form:

- an alcohol called glycerol
- sodium salts or potassium salts of carboxylic acids with long carbon chains.

These salts are the soaps. For example, sodium stearate and potassium stearate are soaps.

Worked example | HIGHER

The active part of a soap is not the sodium ions or potassium ions. Instead, it is the other, main part, which is an anion. Describe and sketch the structure of a soap anion.

hydrophobic tail   hydrophilic head

The 'tail' is hydrophobic. It dissolves in oily dirt or grease.

The 'head' of the anion is hydrophilic. It dissolves in water.

Notice how the scientific words **hydrophilic** and **hydrophobic** are used rather than 'water-loving' and 'water-hating'.

EXAM ALERT!

In a recent examination, some candidates muddled up the words 'hydrophilic' and 'hydrophobic', while others even thought that the soap anion was a living organism.

Students have struggled with this topic in recent exams - **be prepared!**   ResultsPlus

---

How soap works | HIGHER

hydrophobic 'tails' dissolve in the grease and the hydrophilic 'heads' dissolve in the water

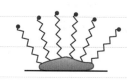

some of the soap anions get beneath the grease and start to lift it off the fabric

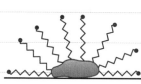

grease leaves the fabric, surrrounded by soap anions

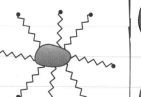

Turning oils into fats | HIGHER

At room temperature, unsaturated oils are liquid and fats are solid. Oils can be converted into fats for use in margarine by catalytic hydrogenation. The oils are reacted with hydrogen gas in the presence of a catalyst. This converts carbon–carbon double bonds in the oils into single bonds.

Now try this

target E-C

1. What type of substance are oils and fats? **(1 mark)**

2. Describe how soaps are produced from oils and fats. **(2 marks)**

3. (a) Describe the structure of a soap anion. **(3 marks)**

    (b) Describe how a soap removes greasy stains from fabric. **(2 marks)**

target C-A

HIGHER

4. Describe how liquid oils can be converted to solid fats. **(2 marks)**

Chemistry extended writing 4

Worked example

The government has recently introduced a minimum charge of 50p per unit for alcohol in Scotland. This has increased the cost of cheap bottles of vodka and other spirits, and should reduce the amount of these drinks that people consume.

Discuss whether this measure to reduce consumption of spirits is a good idea. **(6 marks)**

Sample answer 1

People like to drink because it helps them to relax and enjoy themselves. However, drinking too much is bad for you – especially if you binge drink. And vodka is highly alcoholic too, so drinking it is worse for you. The government wants to keep people healthy, so it's probably a good idea.

This is a basic answer. Although it does make one or two useful points, none of the arguments that it puts forward are developed. There are many more arguments that could be made about the harmful effects of alcohol. The question refers to this change in the law affecting spirits in particular and, although the answer mentions this, it does not explain why this change affects spirits in particular.

Sample answer 2

Vodka – and other spirits – contain large amounts of alcohol. Most spirits are about 40% alcohol. This change in pricing will make cheap vodka more expensive, but probably won't affect drinks like beer. People can misuse alcohol, especially spirits, by binge drinking – drinking large amounts of alcohol to get drunk quickly. This is bad, because alcohol is a drug and is bad for the health in large amounts. It can lead to liver damage and alcohol causes many deaths a year, especially as people are less aware of what they are doing when they are drunk. However, drinking in moderation is not a problem. It can help people enjoy a party and some studies show that small amounts of alcohol are not damaging to health. However, a change that stops people bingeing on cheap drinks is a good thing.

This is an excellent answer. It sums up many of the arguments against cheap alcohol, but also considers some of the arguments on the other side of the argument. It then reaches a conclusion – this is what is expected in a 'discuss' question.

Now try this   HIGHER

1. One stage in the manufacture of nitric acid is the oxidation of ammonia to nitrogen monoxide. The reaction is exothermic in the forward direction.

$$4NH_3(g) + 5O_2(g) \rightleftharpoons 4NO(g) + 6H_2O(g)$$

Use your knowledge of equilibrium reactions to suggest the conditions that might produce the best possible yield for this reaction. **(6 marks)**

You are not expected to give exact reaction conditions – just say whether the temperature / pressure needed is high or low. Don't forget to consider how the reaction conditions affect the time to reach equilibrium.

Chemistry extended writing 5

Worked example

A student has 44 g of dry ice (solid carbon dioxide). She lets the dry ice turn into a gas and blow up a large balloon at room temperature and pressure. She measures the volume of the gas and then passes the gas over hot carbon, until it turns into carbon monoxide.

$$CO_2\ (g) + C\ (s) \rightarrow 2CO\ (g)$$

The student notices that the volume of the gas doubles in this process, but the mass of the gas only increases by 12 g.

Explain the observations that the student makes. (relative atomic masses: C = 12, O = 16)　　**(6 marks)**

Sample answer 1

The mass goes up by 12 g – this is the mass of carbon. You can see in the equation that the carbon dioxide gains a carbon. The volume of the gas goes up because the carbon monoxide is bigger than carbon dioxide.

This is a basic answer. The question gives a series of numerical data, and this answer doesn't really use any of this. It does refer to the equation to give a simple explanation for the increase in mass. The reason for the increase in volume is not correct. Better use of the data and a good explanation for the change in volume would improve this answer.

Sample answer 2

Formula mass of carbon dioxide = 44, so 44 g is 1 mole of carbon dioxide. This means that the gas has a volume of 24 dm³ to start – one mole of any gas has this volume. In the reaction, the carbon dioxide forms twice as much carbon monoxide by reacting with carbon – we can see this by looking at the equation for this reaction. Formula mass of carbon monoxide = 28, so two moles of carbon monoxide = 56 g. This explains that increase of mass of 12 g. As there are two moles of carbon monoxide, the new volume will be 2 × 24 = 48 dm³.

This is an excellent answer. When dealing with the change in mass, this answer calculates correct formula masses of the substances and considers the numbers of moles of substances present. With the data on volumes, this answer gives a good definition of the molar volume of a gas and applies it correctly to this reaction. Finally, it refers back to the equation given in the question.

Now try this

1. The molecules C_3H_6 and C_3H_8 are members of different homologous series.

    Compare the two homologous series to which these molecules belong.　　**(6 marks)**

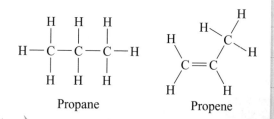

Propane   Propene

Radiation in medicine

Radiation transfers energy from place to place. The term 'radiation' includes all electromagnetic waves and sound waves, and also energy transferred by particles (such as alpha and beta particles).

Medical physics provides doctors with ways to diagnose illnesses as well as treat them.

Diagnostic device	How it works	Advantages	Disadvantages
CAT (CT) Scan (computer aided tomography)	uses X-rays to scan body	✓ detailed images ✓ 3D images can be built up on a computer from sectional scans	✗ expensive equipment ✗ relatively high radiation dose
ultrasound scanner	high-frequency sound waves are reflected by features inside a patient's body	✓ very low risk – allows a real-time image to be viewed	none – widely used in prenatal monitoring
endoscope	uses fibre optics to provide live view of the internal structures in a patient	✓ provided direct, real-time view of internal body tissue ✓ allows keyhole surgery, without the need for major surgery	✗ cannot see through tissues

Intensity and distance

The intensity of radiation is the amount of energy arriving per second over an area of 1 m². Energy spreads out from a source in all directions. The intensity decreases with distance because the radiation is spread over an increasing area.

Worked example

The intensity of the Sun's radiation is about 1.4 kW/m².

(a) Calculate the amount of energy per second from the Sun falling on a roof measuring 12.5 m by 4 m.

(b) In practice the figure may be much lower. Suggest a reason for this.

The formula for calculating intensity is:
intensity (in W/m²) = power (W)/area (m²),
or $I = P/A$

(a) The area of the roof is 12.5 m × 4 m
= 50 m²
$P = I \times A$
$P = 1400$ W × 50 m²
= 70 000 W (70 kW)

(b) As the radiation from the Sun passes through the atmosphere some energy is reflected, absorbed or scattered.

Now try this

1. Jupiter is roughly 5 times more distant from the Sun than the Earth. The intensity of the Sun's radiation at the edge of the Earth's atmosphere is 1.4 kW/m². Explain why the intensity of the Sun's radiation is so much lower at Jupiter's surface. **(3 marks)**

2. A satellite in orbit around the Earth has an array of solar panels that measures 7 m by 2 m. Calculate the maximum electrical power the satellite could obtain from these solar panels. **(2 marks)**

How eyes work

Parts of the eye

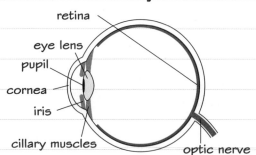

retina
eye lens
pupil
cornea
iris
cillary muscles
optic nerve

You can compare the eye to a video camera, which also has a lens, a hole or aperture that can be varied in size and a screen with electronic sensors where the image is formed. The signals are then transmitted by a cable to be processed by a computer.

Light enters the eye through a hole called the pupil. The cornea and the lens focus the light to form a sharp image on the retina. The nerves in the retina convert the image into electrical signals that are sent to the brain along the optic nerve.

Focusing the image

The eye lens changes shape to produce a sharp image on the retina.

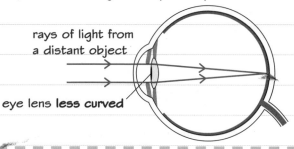

rays of light from a distant object

eye lens **less curved**

rays of light from a near object

eye lens **more curved**

Near and far points

The far point is the most distant point an eye can focus on. For a normal eye, this is infinity. When focusing on very distant objects like the Moon or stars the eye lens is at its thinnest. The near point for a normal eye is the closest point on which the eye can focus. This is about 25 cm for adults with normal vision.

Young people with normal vision can focus on objects closer than 25 cm. 25 cm is an average for the adult population.

Worked example

Lenses that are more curved (fatter) are more powerful – this means that they can bend rays of light through bigger angles. Draw two diagrams to show that as an object gets closer to the eye the lens needs to bend light more to focus it onto the retina.

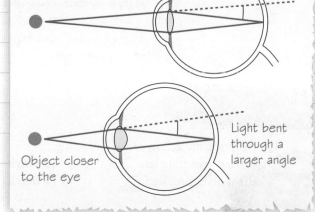

Object closer to the eye

Light bent through a larger angle

Now try this

1. Name the following parts of the eye:
   (a) A hole that allows light to enter the eye. **(1 mark)**
   (b) The coloured part around this hole. **(1 mark)**

target D-C

2. **(a)** State the near point for a person with normal eyesight. **(1 mark)**
   (b) Describe what is meant by the near point. **(1 mark)**

target C-B

HIGHER

Sight problems

Converging and diverging lenses

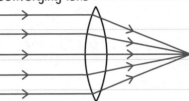

Converging lens

Diverging lens

A converging lens bends rays of light towards one another, bringing them to a point.

A diverging lens bends rays of light away from each other.

Lenses that are thicker in the middle are converging lenses and those that are thinner in the middle are diverging lenses.

Long and short sight

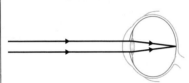 

'Long-sighted' people can focus on distant objects but not near ones.

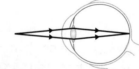 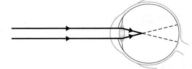

'Short-sighted' people can focus on close objects but not distant ones.

Worked example

What are the causes and symptoms of **(a)** short sight and **(b)** long sight?

(a) A short-sighted person may have eyeballs that are too long, or eye lenses that are too powerful even when the muscles are relaxed. A person with short sight can focus on close objects but not distant ones.

(b) A long-sighted person may have eyeballs that are too short, or eye lenses that are not powerful enough. This often happens as we get older and the lens does not bend enough. A person with long sight can focus on distant objects but not close ones.

Now try this

target
D-C

1. Describe the action of the following:
   (a) a converging lens   **(1 mark)**
   (b) a diverging lens.   **(1 mark)**

2. State how the near and far points are affected for people suffering from the following:
   (a) short-sightedness   **(1 mark)**
   (b) long-sightedness.   **(2 marks)**

Correcting sight problems

Correcting long- and short-sightedness

Spectacles are a simple way of correcting these conditions. If someone is long-sighted this can be corrected by wearing glasses with converging lenses. Short-sightedness is corrected with glasses fitted with diverging lenses.

Long-sightedness

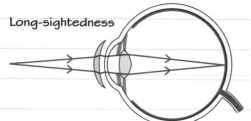

A **converging** lens brings the rays together so light is focused on the retina.

Short-sightedness

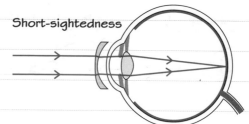

A **diverging** lens makes the rays come together further away, so light is focused on the retina.

The same corrections can be produced with contact lenses.

Worked example

State some advantages and disadvantages of wearing contact lenses.

Advantages – Contact lenses are safe when playing sport because they cannot be knocked off or broken; and people may prefer not to wear glasses.

Disadvantages – Contact lenses must be kept very clean otherwise they can cause eye infections; some people find them uncomfortable to wear.

Laser surgery is a permanent change and means that contact lenses or glasses are no longer needed, but it does involve surgery and it is expensive.

Worked example

HIGHER

Laser surgery is an alternative to wearing glasses or contact lenses. Explain how laser treatment is used to correct problems like long- and short-sightedness.

The patient is given a local anaesthetic. Lasers are used to make small, precise cuts in the cornea. These permanently change the shape of the cornea. Shaping the cornea in this way can make it act like a diverging or converging lens, as required by the patient's condition.

EXAM ALERT!

Questions on lasers can include calculations. A recent question on laser surgery meant that students had to use powers of 10. Only around one out of every six students got full marks. Make sure that you know how to use your calculator to help you in an exam – and take it with you!

Students have struggled with this topic in recent exams - **be prepared!**   ResultsPlus

Now try this

target **D-C**

1. State two ways in which short-sightedness or long-sightedness can be corrected. **(2 marks)**

target **B-A**

HIGHER

2. A surgeon carrying out laser treatment on a patient's eyes changes the shape of the patient's cornea to make it slightly thinner in the middle than towards the edges.

    (a) State how this changes the way light is affected when it passes through the cornea. **(1 mark)**

    (b) State whether the patient is long-sighted or short-sighted. **(1 mark)**

Different lenses

Powerful lenses bend light more and this is related to their shape.

The power of lenses

parallel rays of light all
converge to pass through f.

parallel rays of light diverge so that
they all seem to come from f.

focal length (f) focal length (f) focal length (f) focal length (f)

focal point focal point

The stronger lens on the right is
fatter so it has more sharply curved faces
and has a shorter focal length.

The weaker lens on the right is
thinner so it has less curved faces
and has a longer focal length.

The power of a lens is given by the formula:

$$\text{power (dioptres, D)} = \frac{1}{\text{Focal length (metres)}}$$

Use the reciprocal button on your calculator to help with calculations of power. **Remember** that the focal length must be converted to metres to give power in the correct unit (dioptres).

Worked example

Calculate the power of the following lenses.

(a) A converging lens of focal length 25 cm.

(b) A diverging lens of focal length 20 cm.

Don't forget to convert centimetres to metres when using the lens power equation.

We use a minus sign to show that the focal length and the power are for a diverging lens.

(a) $25\,\text{cm} = 0.25\,\text{m}$

$$\text{power} = \frac{1}{\text{focal length}}$$

$$\text{power} = \frac{1}{0.25}$$

$$= +4\,\text{D}$$

(b) This is a diverging lens so $f = -20\,\text{cm}$

$$= -0.2\,\text{m}$$

$$\text{power} = \frac{-1}{0.2}$$

$$= -5\,\text{D}$$

Now try this

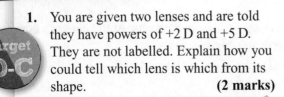

1. You are given two lenses and are told they have powers of +2 D and +5 D. They are not labelled. Explain how you could tell which lens is which from its shape. **(2 marks)**

2. Calculate the focal length of a converging lens with a power of +1 D. **(3 marks)**

HIGHER

The lens equation

HIGHER This whole page covers Higher material.

The position of the image formed by a lens can be calculated using the following formula:

$$\frac{1}{f} = \frac{1}{u} + \frac{1}{v}$$

f = focal length, u = object distance, v = image distance

Real is positive

Lenses can form images that can be focused onto a screen. These are called real images. The image viewed through a magnifying glass appears to be behind the lens and cannot be focused onto a screen. This is called a virtual image.

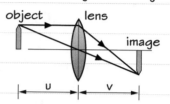

A lens forming a real image

f is positive for converging lenses, and negative for diverging lenses. If the lens equation gives a negative value for the image distance, v, this tells you that the image is virtual. A virtual image cannot be formed on a screen.

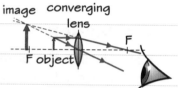

A lens forming a virtual image

Worked example

A converging lens is used to project an image of the filament of a lamp onto a screen. The distance from the filament to the lens is 12.5 cm. The lens has a focal length of 10 cm. Calculate the distance between the screen and the lens when the image of the filament is sharp.

$f = +10$ cm, $u = 12.5$ cm

$$\frac{1}{u} + \frac{1}{v} = \frac{1}{f}$$

$$\frac{1}{12.5} + \frac{1}{v} = \frac{1}{10}$$

$$\frac{1}{v} = \frac{1}{10} - \frac{1}{12.5}$$

$$= \frac{10}{100} - \frac{8}{100}$$

$$= \frac{2}{100} = \frac{1}{50}$$

$v = 50$ cm

> Your calculator may be able to do this for you using the reciprocal or inverse key.

> It does not matter what the units for the distance are here as long as they are all the same.

Now try this

1. State what type of image is formed in the following situations.

target C-B

   (a) A lens is used as a burning glass (to set fire to paper using the Sun's rays). **(1 mark)**

   (b) A lens is used to project an image onto a cinema screen. **(1 mark)**

   (c) A lens is used to magnify small print in a book. **(1 mark)**

2. The average human eye has a diameter of 25 mm.

target A-A*

   (a) Explain whether the eye lens shape should be at its fattest or its thinnest when viewing a distant object. **(3 marks)**

   (b) Calculate what strength the eye lens should have when reading a book placed at the average near point of vision (25 cm). **(5 marks)**

Reflection and refraction

Reflection

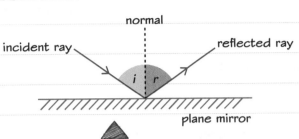

normal

incident ray — reflected ray

i r

plane mirror

The **normal** is a line drawn at 90° to the mirror surface at the point that the arriving or incident ray meets the mirror. The angles *i* and *r* are measured from this line.

The law of reflection is   angle *i* = angle *r*

When sketching ray diagrams you do not need to get the angles exactly right, but the sketch should not appear to ignore the rule. If you are asked to *plot* a ray diagram, use a protractor to measure the angles.

Refraction

Refraction is the change in the direction of a light ray that happens when it travels from one transparent material into another. Notice that the ray of light bends *towards* the normal as it enters the glass and *away* from the normal when it leaves the glass.

air   glass block

refracted ray — normal

normal — r

i

incident ray

Rays of light that meet a surface at 90° do not bend at all but simply continue into the material without a change in direction.

Refraction and wave speed

Refraction happens because light waves travel at different speeds in different materials. Light waves travel more slowly in glass than they do in air.

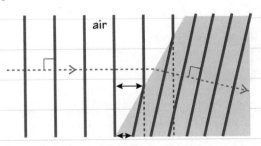

air

The red lines are waves and the dotted purple arrows show the direction that the light rays are travelling. When the waves travel from air into a denser material like glass they travel more slowly. The dotted red lines show how far the waves would have travelled in air but as they travel at a lower speed in glass the direction is turned through an angle. The size of this angle depends on how much the wave has been slowed down. Wavelength also changes.

Now try this

1. Draw a labelled diagram to show how a ray of light is reflected from a mirror surface. **(2 marks)**

    target
    D-C

2. **(a)** Explain, with the aid of a clear diagram, why light waves change direction as they travel across a boundary between air and glass. **(3 marks)**

    target
    C-A

    HIGHER **(b)** State when a light ray will not change direction. **(1 mark)**

Critical angle

The law of refraction HIGHER

The law of refraction, called Snell's Law, is $n = \dfrac{\sin i}{\sin r}$

A denser medium is one in which light travels more slowly than in air, like glass, water or perspex. The bigger the refractive index of a material, the more it slows down light.

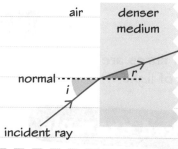

Total internal reflection

Worked example

A ray of light hits a glass block with an angle of incidence of 40°. Some of it is reflected and some passes into the glass block. The glass has a refractive index of 1.5.

Calculate the angle of refraction.

Rearrange the formula to give
$r = \sin^{!} \dfrac{\sin 40°}{1.5} \rightarrow r = 25.4°$

Total internal reflection can take place with sound as well as light.

The critical angle can be calculated using the following formula: $\sin c = 1/n$

The value of the critical angle depends on the refractive index of the material. The bigger n is, the smaller the value of the critical angle.

Total internal reflection can only occur when light travelling from a dense material like glass meets a boundary with a less dense material like air.

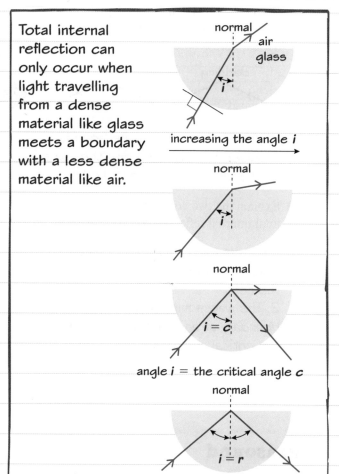

increasing the angle i

angle i = the critical angle c

total internal reflection
angle i > critical angle c

Worked example   HIGHER

A type of glass has a refractive index of 1.6. Calculate the critical angle for this type of glass.

$\sin c = \dfrac{1}{n}$

$\sin c = \dfrac{1}{1.6} = 0.625$

then use a calculator: $c = \sin^{-1} (0.625)$
to obtain $c = 38.7°$ (1 d.p.)

Now try this

target
B–A
HIGHER

1. The refractive index of glass is 1.5. A ray of light meets the surface of a block of this glass at an angle of 50° to the normal. Calculate the angle of refraction.

    (3 marks)

2. The refractive index of diamond is 2.42. Calculate the critical angle for diamond.

    (3 marks)

Using reflection and refraction

Optical fibres are thin glass fibres that are used to transmit digital data in the form of pulses of light. The light travels along the fibres by total internal reflection.

Worked example

(a) Draw a labelled diagram to explain how total internal reflection (TIR) is used in optical fibres.

(a)

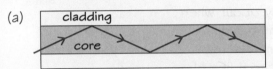

Rays of light meeting the boundary between the cladding and the core are totally internally reflected.

(b) Explain the two conditions necessary for total internal reflection to take place.

(b) 1. The cladding must have a smaller refractive index (lower density) than the core.
2. The waves must meet the boundary at an angle greater than the critical angle.

EXAM ALERT!

If you are asked to complete a ray diagram make sure that you do it accurately. Draw straight lines and the correct angles. A recent exam question which asked students to complete a ray diagram was only correctly completed by half the students.

Students have struggled with this topic in recent exams - **be prepared!** Result Plus

Endoscopes

Endoscopes can be used to look inside patients' bodies, and make use of optical fibres. Endoscopes allow 'keyhole' surgery. This is surgery conducted through a very small cut in the body to speed up recovery time.

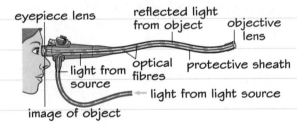

Ultrasound

Ultrasound is sound with a much higher frequency than can be heard by humans. It can travel through human tissue without causing damage, so it is used to scan the body. Some ultrasound is reflected whenever there is a change in the speed of the ultrasound waves. A computer builds up an image from the reflected and refracted ultrasound waves.

Ultrasound of a different frequency and intensity is used to break up stones that form in parts of the body without the need for surgery. Ultrasound is also used to treat muscle and other soft tissue injuries by focusing energy on the specific injury location.

Now try this

1. Describe two uses of ultrasound in modern medicine.   **(2 marks)**

2. Describe how optical fibres are used in the construction of endoscopes used in 'keyhole' surgery.   **(3 marks)**

Physics extended writing 1

To answer an extended writing question successfuly you need to:

✓ use your scientific knowledge to answer the question

✓ organise your answer so that it is logical and well ordered

✓ use full sentences in your writing and make sure that your spelling, punctuation and grammar are correct.

Worked example

The human eye can suffer from a number of conditions, which often means that a person's vision needs to be corrected. Two of the most common problems are when people are either 'short-sighted' or 'long-sighted'.

Explain how an optician can correct these conditions so that a person can clearly see objects that are both nearby and far away. Refer to the structure of the eye and the way that lenses behave in your answer.

(6 marks)

Sample answer 1

A person who is short-sighted cannot see things far away, whereas a person who is long-sighted cannot see things close up. This is corrected for by using glasses or contact lenses so that you can see things properly.

This is a basic answer. What it says is correct, but it does not provide the detail required. Refraction is not mentioned; nor is any detail about the structure of the eye and the causes of long and short sight.

Sample answer 2

When a person is long-sighted, the rays of light entering the eye are not refracted as much as they should be and the light rays from a close object converge at a point beyond the retina. This happens because the ciliary muscles cannot make the lens in the eye as thick as it needs to be. This means that the lens has too little power and there is not enough refraction of the incoming light. When a person is short-sighted, the rays of light from a distant object converge at a point in front of the retina because the lens is too powerful. In both cases, the person sees a blurred image. To correct long sight, an optician will use convex or converging lenses to bend light inwards. To correct short sight, diverging lenses are used. Simple glass lenses in spectacles, or contact lenses which float on the eye, can both be used to correct these problems with vision. Both solutions mean that light rays converge on the retina to produce a sharp image, with the near point now being at 25 cm and the far point being at infinity.

This is an excellent, detailed answer, referring to the structure of the eye and the nature of refraction. Short sight and long sight are both explained in detail and with the correct use of physics terminology. Spelling, punctuation and grammar are of a very high quality.

Now try this

1. Opticians can correct problems with vision by using laser treatment. Compare this treatment with the use of contact lenses or glasses.

(6 marks)

X-rays

X-rays are electromagnetic waves with a very short wavelength. They are able to penetrate soft body tissue. We can use them to produce images of the bones and organs within the human body.

X-rays

As X-rays pass through body tissue they can be absorbed by molecules, and the molecules become ionised. In this process the X-rays lose energy and eventually cannot ionise any more tissue.

Worked example

Explain how ionisation by X-rays is related to their frequency.

Higher-frequency X-rays are more ionising. This is because they transfer more energy then those with lower frequency.

Producing X-rays

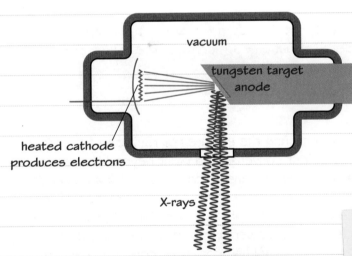

vacuum

tungsten target anode

heated cathode produces electrons

X-rays

In an X-ray machine electrons are produced by a cathode, which is heated by a filament inside an evacuated tube (a vacuum tube). The electrons accelerate towards an anode because of the very high potential difference between the anode and the cathode. Embedded in the anode is a tungsten target and when very energetic electrons strike the target some of this energy is converted into X-rays.

The vacuum means there are no gas molecules to scatter and absorb the energy of electrons striking the target.

Remember that the anode is positive and the cathode is negative.

The beam in an X-ray machine consists of large numbers of electrons travelling from the cathode to the tungsten target. Since electrons carry charge, the beam provides a current through the vacuum in the X-ray tube.

Now try this

1. Explain what happens to the energy of an X-ray as it passes through body tissue. **(2 marks)**

   target **C-B** HIGHER

2. (a) Describe how X-rays are produced in an X-ray machine. **(3 marks)**

   target **B-A*** HIGHER

   (b) Only a small amount of the energy used in an X-ray machine is converted into X-rays. Suggest what form the rest of the energy is converted into. **(1 mark)**

X-ray calculations

Current in beams of charged particles

The size of the current in an X-ray tube is given by the formula: $I = N \times q$

I = current (ampere, A)

N = number of particles per second (1/second, 1/s)

q = charge carried by each electron (coulomb, C)

EXAM ALERT!

Make sure you can use this equation and understand it. A recent question on this equation led to about a third of all students getting no marks at all.

Students have struggled with this topic in recent exams - **be prepared!**

 ResultsPlus

Worked example   HIGHER

A typical beam current in an X-ray machine is 1 mA. An electron has a charge of 1.6×10^{-19} C. Calculate the number of electrons that strike the target each second.

Use your calculator for questions like this.

$1\,mA = 0.001\ A\ or\ 1 \times 10^{-3}\ A$

$N = \dfrac{I}{q}$

$= (1 \times 10^{-3}\ A)/(1.6 \times 10^{-19}\ C)$

$= 6.25 \times 10^{15}$ electrons strike the target per second

---

The kinetic energy of particles in beams   HIGHER

In an X-ray electron beam the electrons gain kinetic energy as they are accelerated through the vacuum by the potential difference. The unit of potential difference is the volt. One coulomb of electric charge gains one joule of energy when it is accelerated through a potential difference of one volt.

$KE = e \times V$ KE = kinetic energy (joules, J)

e = charge on the electron (coulomb, C)

V = accelerating potential difference (volts, V)

Kinetic energy can also be calculated using the formula:

$KE = \frac{1}{2}mv^2$ m = mass of electron (kg)

v = velocity of electron (m/s)

Take care not to confuse v (which is velocity) and V (which is volts).

So $e \times V = \frac{1}{2}mv^2$

Now try this

1. State what happens to the number of electrons striking the target in an X-ray machine if the beam current is doubled.   **(1 mark)**

HIGHER

The mass of an electron is 9.1×10^{-31} kg.

2. An X-ray machine has a potential difference of 30 kV between the cathode and the anode. (In the following questions electron charge, e = 1.6×10^{-19} C and electron mass, m = 9.1×10^{-31} kg.)

HIGHER

(a) Calculate the energy gained by an electron as it travels from the cathode to the anode.   **(2 marks)**

(b) How fast will the electron be moving when it hits the anode?   **(2 marks)**

Using X-rays

When electromagnetic radiation, such as light, spreads out from a source its energy is spread out over an area which increases with distance.

The inverse square law

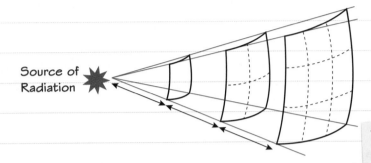

Area increases with the square of distance so intensity decreases with the square of distance. For example, at twice the distance from the source the intensity is one quarter as much because the area is four times greater.

Source of Radiation

This rule applies to any energy source, including all EM radiation and sound.

Absorption of X-rays

Worked example

Suggest why the edges of bones look whiter than the middles in X-rays. Include a sketch in your answer.

Bones are hollow, and most of the X-rays are absorbed by the denser bone around the outside. X-rays pass through more bone at the edges.

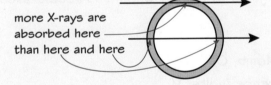

more X-rays are absorbed here than here and here

CAT scans and fluoroscopes

Conventional X-rays produce a 2-dimensional image of a patient.

In a CAT scanner an X-ray source is used to produce a 3-dimensional image of the internal structure of a patient.

Fluoroscopes use X-ray images on a screen. These allow doctors to see a real-time image of a patient's internal condition.

Increasing the thickness of the material increases the X-rays absorbed.

Risks and benefits of X-rays in medicine

Risks	Benefits
✗ X-rays can kill and damage living cells.	✓ X-rays can help to give a reliable diagnosis and make sure treatment is fast and accurate.
✗ Risks are greater for babies and young children, so exposure is kept to a minimum.	✓ X-rays are non-invasive. (This means that the patient does not have to have an operation to see what is happening in their body.)

Now try this

target E-D

1. State one factor that reduces the amount of X-rays that pass through an object. **(1 mark)**

target D-B

2. Describe the advantages and disadvantages of CAT scans compared with conventional X-rays. **(4 marks)**

ECGs and pacemakers

Action potentials are electrical signals that control the heart muscles. They are generated by the heart's natural pacemaker to make the heart beat at the correct rate to supply the body with the oxygen it needs. An ECG (electrocardiogram) measures the changing electrical signals in the heart.

Action potentials and ECGs

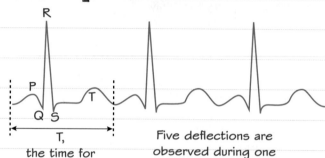

the time for one complete heart beat

Five deflections are observed during one heart beat, labelled PQRST as shown.

An ECG can show if a heartbeat is abnormal and can allow doctors to diagnose problems with a patient's heart. An abnormal heartbeat may be irregular or have an unusual rhythm, for example unusual deflections like a prolonged ST complex.

Heart/pulse rate

A normal ECG shows the heart beating regularly. The pulse rate is the frequency of this signal.

$$f = \frac{1}{T}$$ f = frequency (hertz, Hz) and T = time period (seconds, s)

The pulse rate is usually given in beats per minute, so the frequency given by this formula must be multiplied by 60 to give a pulse in beats per minute. The average resting pulse rate for an adult is about 72 beats per minute.

Worked example

Describe the purpose of an artificial pacemaker.

A pacemaker is used to monitor the heart and detect irregular heartbeats. If an irregular heartbeat is detected the pacemaker produces electrical signals to correct the heart rate.

Pulse oximetry

Pulse oximeters measure the amount of oxygen in the blood. They also measure the pulse rate.

Two light sources. One is infrared and one is visible red light. Blood carrying a lot of oxygen (oxygenated blood) absorbs more infrared light because it is a different colour from deoxygenated blood. This difference allows the amount of oxygen in the blood to be calculated.

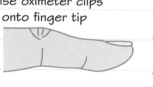

pulse oximeter clips onto finger tip

to processor/computer

two light detectors

Now try this

target **C-A**

HIGHER

1. A patient's ECG shows that the time between heartbeats is 0.6 s. Calculate the patient's heart rate in beats per minute.
   (2 marks)

2. (a) What does a pulse oximeter measure?
   (2 marks)

   (b) Explain how a pulse oximeter works.
   (2 marks)

Properties of radiation

The nuclei of some elements are unstable. The nuclei change and emit particles or waves. These types of emissions are shown in the table.

Type of radiation emitted	Relative charge	Relative mass	Ionising power	Penetrating power	Affected by magnetic fields?
alpha, α (helium nucleus, two protons and two neutrons)	+2	4	heavily ionising	very low, only ~10 cm in air	yes
beta, β− (an electron from the nucleus)	−1	1/1840	weakly ionising	low, stopped by thin aluminium	yes, but in the opposite direction to α and β+
positron, β+ (a particle with same size as electron but an opposite charge)	+1	1/1840	weakly ionising	low, stopped by thin aluminium	yes
neutron, n	0	1	not directly ionising	high	no, since neither are charged
gamma, γ (waves)	0	0	not directly ionising	very high, stopped only by thick lead	

You do not have to know the actual mass or charge of atomic particles. Protons and neutrons have nearly identical mass, given as a relative value of 1. Electrons are very much smaller and their relative mass is often taken as zero. It should be remembered that they do have a tiny mass (approximately 1/1840 the mass of a proton). Similarly, the charge on a proton is a positive charge and the electron has an equal amount of negative charge.

EXAM ALERT!

You should be able to apply the properties of different forms of radioactivity to their uses. A recent question that asked pupils to do this was only fully answered by one in every 200 students!

Students have struggled with this topic in recent exams - **be prepared!** ResultsPlus

Worked example

Explain why an atom has a neutral charge.

An atom has the same number of protons and electrons. This means it has the same number of positive charges and negative charges, so the atom is neutral.

Now try this

target D-C

1. Describe the properties of three types of radiation that may be emitted from a radioactive substance. **(3 marks)**

target A-A*
HIGHER

2. The activity from a radioactive source is measured with a Geiger counter. The count rate is not affected when a thin piece of cardboard is placed between the source and the counter. When a 1 millimetre thick sheet of aluminium is placed between the source and the counter, the count rate drops, but it does not drop to the level of naturally occurring radiation (the background count). Explain the types of radiation emitted by the radioactive source. **(3 marks)**

Balancing nuclear equations

Beta decay [HIGHER]

In β^- decay a neutron within an unstable nucleus decays to give a proton and an electron; this electron is emitted at high speed as a beta particle.

In β^+ decay a proton in the nucleus decays to a neutron and a positron; the positron is ejected from the nucleus at high speed carrying +1 charge away but having almost no effect on the mass of the nucleus.

Changes to the nucleus

Type of radiation emitted	Effect on the mass of the nucleus	Effect on the charge of the nucleus
alpha α	nuclear mass reduced by 4 [−4]	positive charge reduced by 2 [−2]
beta $\beta-$	no change [0]	positive charge increased by 1 [+1]
beta $\beta+$	no change [0]	positive charge reduced by 1 [−1]
gamma	the emission of gamma radiation has no effect on either the mass or the overall charge of a nucleus	

Balancing nuclear equations [HIGHER]

In any radioactive decay the total relative mass and charge stay the same, so the masses and charges on each side of the equation must balance.

Note that the atomic mass numbers at the top must balance: 121 = 121 + 0; and the atomic numbers at the bottom must also add up: 53 = 52 + 1.

Worked example

Balance the nuclear equations for these decays:

(a) Iodine-121 undergoes $\beta+$ decay to form tellurium.

$$^{121}_{53}\text{I} \rightarrow {}^{121}_{52}\text{Te} + {}^{0}_{+1}e$$

$^{0}_{+1}e$ is the emitted $\beta+$ particle.

(b) An isotope of carbon undergoes $\beta-$ decay to form nitrogen-14.

$$^{14}_{6}\text{C} \rightarrow {}^{14}_{7}\text{N} + {}^{0}_{-1}e$$

$^{0}_{-1}e$ is the emitted $\beta-$ particle.

(c) Radon-220 undergoes α decay to form an isotope of polonium.

$$^{220}_{86}\text{Rn} \rightarrow {}^{216}_{84}\text{Rn} + {}^{4}_{2}\text{He}$$

$^{4}_{2}\text{He}$ is the emitted α particle.

Now try this

 target E-D

1. A helium nucleus is represented by the symbol $^{4}_{2}\text{He}$. Explain how this shows the number of protons and neutrons in a helium nucleus. **(3 marks)**

 target B-A

2. Complete the following nuclear equation showing the decay of radium-226 by alpha emission.

$$^{226}_{88}\text{Ra} \rightarrow {}^{222}_{86}\text{Rn} + {}^{4}_{2}\text{He}$$ **(2 marks)**

[HIGHER]

 target B-A* [HIGHER]

3. The radioactive isotope carbon-14 decays by emitting a $\beta-$ particle to the stable isotope of nitrogen, $^{14}_{7}\text{N}$.

(a) Complete this symbol for the radioactive form of carbon $^{\square}_{6}\text{C}$. **(1 mark)**

(b) Write a balanced nuclear equation for this decay process. **(2 marks)**

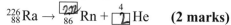

83

The nuclear stability curve

HIGHER This whole page covers Higher material.

The graph shows the N-Z curve for isotopes of all the elements. This shows the ratio between the number of neutrons (N) and the number of protons (Z) in the nucleus.

The ratio of protons to neutrons for stable isotopes is roughly 1 to 1 initially and the blue band on the N-Z curve shows the stable isotopes.

Isotopes that lie off the blue line are unstable and will undergo radioactive decay. The type of decay depends on where the isotope is on the N-Z graph. The decay will result in another isotope being produced with a N:Z ratio closer to 1:1.

> Alpha decay involves the isotope losing 2 neutrons and 2 protons, which means that the isotope formed will be closer to the blue stability line.

> The blue line shows stable isotopes. All isotopes with atomic numbers (Z) greater than 82 are unstable.

> β^- particles are produced when a neutron in the nucleus of the isotope decays to a proton as it emits an electron. This increases Z by one and reduces N by one with the result that the N:Z ratio moves toward the stability curve.

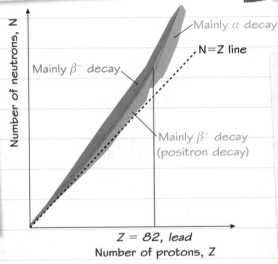

> β^+ particles are produced when a proton in the nucleus of the isotope decays to a neutron by emitting a positron. This decreases Z by one and increases N by one with the result that the N:Z ratio moves toward the stability line.

Worked example

An isotope of uranium has 146 neutrons and 92 protons. **(a)** Explain what kind of radioactive decay is likely to occur. **(b)** Explain what the structure of the new nucleus will be after this decay.

> Remember that any decay that involves a change in the number of protons in the nucleus means that the element has changed to a different element.

(a) Alpha decay, as most isotopes with atomic number greater than 82 decay by emitting an alpha particle.

(b) An alpha particle consists of 2 neutrons and 2 protons so the nucleus formed by alpha decay will have 144 neutrons and 90 protons.

Now try this

target
B-A

1. The radioactive element astatine has 85 protons in its nucleus. Explain what type of decay it is likely to undergo.
(2 marks)

2. Most of the lighter elements have stable isotopes that lie either on or close to the N=Z line. Carbon 14 has 6 protons and 8 neutrons.
   (a) State its N:Z ratio. **(1 mark)**
   (b) Explain what type of decay it is likely to undergo. **(2 marks)**

Quarks 1

HIGHER This whole page covers Higher material.

Up and down quarks

Scientists have shown that the fundamental building blocks of matter are particles called quarks. Protons and neutrons are made up of combinations of two types of quark, called up quarks and down quarks:

up quarks are positively charged
$+\frac{2}{3}e$

down quarks are negatively charged
$-\frac{1}{3}e$

Quarks in protons and neutrons

Protons and neutrons are made of combinations of three quarks.

The proton consists of two up quarks and one down quark.
$+\frac{2}{3}e +\frac{2}{3}e -\frac{1}{3}e = +1e$

The neutron consists of one up quark and two down quarks.
$-\frac{1}{3}e -\frac{1}{3}e +\frac{2}{3}e = 0$

> The unit of charge is the electron charge, e. The proton charge is the same amount of charge as the electron charge, but positive.

These combinations of quarks give the proton and the neutron almost identical mass. The relative atomic mass of both the proton and neutron is 1. Each type of quark has one third of the mass of a proton.

Worked example

A particle consists of one up quark and two down quarks.

(a) Calculate the relative mass and charge on the particle.

(b) State the name of the particle.

(a) All up and down quarks have a mass of $\frac{1}{3}$ of a proton or neutron. So 3 up and down quarks have a total relative mass of 1 (udd).

Charge on 1 up quark = $+\frac{2}{3}e$; Charge on 2 down quarks = $2 \times -\frac{1}{3}e = -\frac{2}{3}e$

Total charge = 0

(b) The particle is a neutron.

Now try this

1. State the arrangement of quarks in the following particles:

target **D-C**

  (a) a proton   **(1 mark)**

  (b) a neutron.   **(1 mark)**

2. (a) Explain why protons and neutrons must be made up of three quarks.

target **C-B**

       (1 mark)

  (b) A hypothetical particle consists of three up quarks. Calculate its charge and relative mass.   **(2 marks)**

Quarks 2

HIGHER This whole page covers Higher material.

Beta minus and beta plus decay are both explained in terms of changes in the quarks in the nucleus.

Beta minus decay

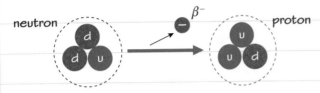

A down quark in a neutron changes into an up quark emitting a β^- and resulting in a proton.

Electric charge is conserved in this process, as the total charge before and after the decay is unchanged. The neutron is neutral overall, and after the decay a $\beta-$ (electron) and a proton are formed.

Beta plus decay

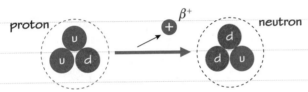

An up quark in a proton changes into an down quark emitting a β^+ and resulting in a neutron.

Again charge is conserved in this decay process.

Worked example

An atom of caesium-137 has 55 protons in its nucleus. Inside the nucleus, a down quark turns into an up quark.

(a) Explain which type of particle the quark was in, and what type of decay this causes.

(b) Describe the changes to the nucleus of the atom.

(a) A down quark turns into an up quark when a neutron changes into a proton. A β^- particle is emitted.

(b) The atomic number increases to 56, as a neutron has changed to a proton. The mass number does not change.

Now try this

target **C-B**

1. Describe the change in the quark structure of a neutron that decays by emitting a β^- particle. **(1 mark)**

target **B-A***

2. Sodium-22 decays to neon-22 by emitting a positron.
   (a) State the effect of positron decay on the atomic number of the decaying atom. **(1 mark)**
   (b) In this process a quark in a proton in a sodium-22 nucleus changes from one type to another. Describe the changes that happen in the nucleus. **(3 marks)**

Dangers of ionising radiation

Destroying living cells

All types of ionising radiation can kill cells. If small numbers of cells are killed the organism can recover by replacing the destroyed cells. If large numbers of cells are destroyed by exposure to large doses of ionising radiation, then the organism cannot recover. Radiation of all types can also cause burns.

Cell mutation

Ionising radiation can also cause mutations in the DNA in cells. In this case the ionising radiation does not kill the cell but makes it work in a different way. One such change may cause the cell to grow uncontrollably, forming a tumour (cancer).

Safe handling of radioactive materials

Danger from exposure is reduced by wearing protective clothing (such as lead aprons), increasing the distance from the source for ionising electromagnetic radiation (such as X-rays) and reducing the length of any exposure.

> The intensity of radiation decreases with the distance from the source, as mentioned on pages 66 and 78.

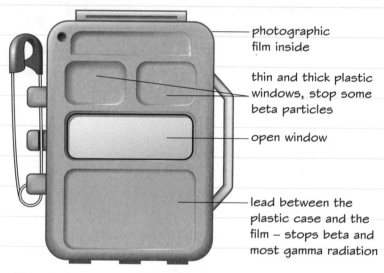

- photographic film inside
- thin and thick plastic windows, stop some beta particles
- open window
- lead between the plastic case and the film – stops beta and most gamma radiation

This dosimeter is a film badge used to monitor the radiation received by its wearer.

Worked example

Describe two precautions taken by dentists and dental nurses to reduce their exposure to ionising radiation while taking an X-ray.

1. They go out of the room in which the X-ray is taking place.
2. They keep the X-ray pulse as short as possible. (This also minimises the patient's exposure.)

Now try this

target D-C

1. Explain how a dosimeter is used and why it is used. **(3 marks)**

target B-A
HIGHER

2. Alpha particles are strongly ionising but have a short range in air and can only penetrate a millimetre or two of living tissue.
   (a) Explain why radioactive gases that emit alpha particles are particularly dangerous. **(2 marks)**
   (b) Suggest a suitable precaution that can be taken to reduce this danger.
   (1 mark)

Radiation in hospitals

Ethics

The use of radioactive materials in the diagnosis and treatment of illness has unwanted and unpleasant side effects. Ethical use means that doctors must inform patients of the adverse effects and the benefits of different types of treatment. Both doctors and their patients must be able to assess whether the benefits and the likelihood of successful treatment outweigh the adverse effects on the patient during and after treatment.

Palliative care

Some medical conditions are untreatable and some will result in the patient dying. Palliative care involves minimising the suffering caused by the condition. For example, radiation can be used to shrink tumours. Ethics require consideration of the quality of life of the patient during palliative treatment.

Questions about this section of the specification will only test your understanding of the terms. You will not be asked to come to conclusions about any particular procedures without being given the information you need.

Worked example

Explain why some radiation treatments for tumours are applied internally and some externally.

Some radiation treatments involve beaming X-rays or gamma rays into the patient from an external machine, but this can destroy healthy tissue as well as cancers.

If the patient takes radioactive materials internally the radiation can be targeted at the tumour and damage to surrounding tissue is reduced. An example of this is the use of radioactive isotopes of iodine to target the thyroid gland in treatment of thyroid conditions.

The radioactive isotope of iodine is absorbed by the thyroid gland in exactly the same way as the stable isotope – this concentrates the radiation dose where it is needed.

PET scanners and tracers

PET scanners are used to produce three-dimensional colour images of the patient's insides. These images help doctors to diagnose and locate health problems. A patient is given a radioactive tracer either by injection or by mouth. The tracer is a radioactive material that decays quickly by emitting positrons. The gamma rays emitted when the positrons mutually annihilated by electrons are detected by the PET scanner and a computer image is produced.

Specific types of tracer are used to target particular locations in the body.

The isotope used as a tracer is often produced in a particle accelerator called a cyclotron. As the tracers decay very quickly it is necessary to produce them close to the hospital where the PET scan is carried out.

Now try this

1. Explain what is meant by palliative care. **(2 marks)**

target D-C

2. A doctor wants to conduct a treatment on a patient to test it out. The likelihood of a successful outcome is very small. Explain why this may be considered unethical. **(3 marks)**

target B-A
HIGHER

Physics extended writing 2

Worked example

X-rays are used in hospitals for diagnosing illnesses and for treating patients. Describe the production and use of X-rays in hospitals, including the precautions that a radiographer would need to take. **(6 marks)**

Sample answer 1

X-rays are produced by an X-ray machine. They have no charge and travel at the speed of light. A radiographer would make sure that they are safe by staying as far away as possible from the X-rays and by wearing protective clothes.

This is a basic answer. What it says is correct, but there is not enough detail about how the X-rays are produced and how distance, exposure time and shielding ensure that the radiographer is not placed at too high a risk. The information in the answer about charge and speed is correct, but not relevant to the question being asked.

Sample answer 2

X-rays are made when high-energy electrons are accelerated and made to collide with a metal target. The electrons are produced by thermionic emission, which means they are released from a heated negative filament (the cathode) and then fired towards the positively charged metal anode. There has to be a vacuum between the anode and cathode to make sure that the X-rays are not absorbed before they hit the target. When the electrons reach the metal target, they are decelerated very quickly, and X-rays are produced.

In order to ensure that they are not exposed to X-rays, radiographers make sure the exposure time is as short as possible. They make sure that they are as far away from the X-rays as possible, because X-rays spread out and their strength decreases as you get further from the source. They can also protect themselves by wearing a lead apron, as dense materials such as lead will absorb X-rays. Sensitive detectors can also be placed in the room so the workers can be warned about any unusually high levels of radiation emitted from the X-ray machine.

This is an excellent answer. It describes the production of X-rays in depth and it gives a detailed explanation of what precautions the radiographer needs to take.

Now try this   HIGHER

1. Compare the use of X-rays and CAT scans for treatment and diagnosis in medicine. **(6 marks)**

Physics extended writing 3

Unstable nuclei can become more stable by emitting alpha or beta particles. Describe the processes of α, β^- and β^+ decay. Refer to the letters on the graph in your answer. **(6 marks)**

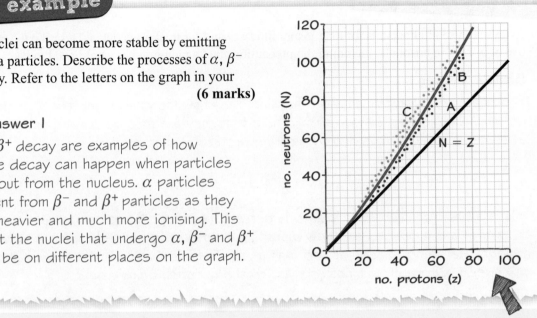

Sample answer 1

α, β^- and β^+ decay are examples of how radioactive decay can happen when particles are given out from the nucleus. α particles are different from β^- and β^+ particles as they are much heavier and much more ionising. This means that the nuclei that undergo α, β^- and β^+ decay will be on different places on the graph.

This does not contain enough information to answer any part of the question. It states what the question is and then adds some information about α particles, which hasn't been asked for in the question, and so will not get any marks. There is no correct explanation of where particles that undergo α, β^- or β^+ decay are to be found on the graph.

Sample answer 2

β^- particles are high-energy electrons that are emitted from unstable nuclei that have too many neutrons. During this type of decay, a neutron turns into a proton and the β^- particle is ejected from the nucleus. β^+ decay occurs when a nucleus has too many protons. This time a proton decays into a neutron and the β^+ particle is emitted.

Alpha particle decay happens at position A on the graph, above $Z = 82$, as losing two neutrons and two protons lets the heavy, unstable nuclei move into the stable band. Isotopes that are below or to the right of the curve of stable isotopes will undergo β^+ decay to reduce the number of protons in the nucleus. This will occur at position B. β^- decay will occur when the nuclei need to reduce the number of neutrons to move into the stable band. This will occur for isotopes that are found above or to the right of the stable isotopes curve as shown by the letter C.

This is an excellent answer. It correctly describes the processes of α, β^- and β^+ decay and correctly identifies where the nuclei that undergo α, β^- and β^+ decay would be found on the graph. Spelling, punctuation and grammar are good, the answer is organised well and correct scientific words are used.

Now try this HIGHER

1. Protons and neutrons are composed of smaller particles called quarks. Describe the changes that take place in β^- and β^+ decay by referring to the quarks present in protons and neutrons. **(6 marks)**

Particle accelerators

Particle accelerators help scientists find out more about the subatomic particles that the world is made up of.

Circular motion and cyclotrons

To make any object move in a circular path it must have a force acting on it towards the centre of the path – this is called a centripetal force. In a cyclotron this centripetal force is caused by a strong magnetic field acting on the charged particle.

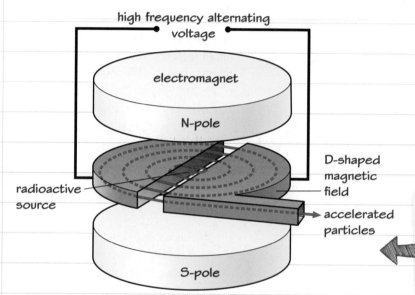

Electrons are fired into the centre of one of the D-shaped enclosures, and a strong magnetic field defelects the electrons so that they follow the curved path shown. As they cross the gap from one D electrode to the other a large voltage makes them accelerate. Eventually the electrons emerge at very high speed and very large kinetic energy.

Charged particles moving in a magnetic field experience a force at right angles to their direction of travel and this makes the particles move in a circular path.

Making radioactive isotopes

Stable isotopes can be made radioactive by using a cyclotron to fire high energy particles at their nuclei. For example, xenon gas can be bombarded with protons to make the radioactive isotope iodine-131. This iodine is used in the treatment and diagnosis of conditions affecting the thyroid gland.

Radioactive isotopes are often used in medicine.

Worked example

State two reasons why scientists work collaboratively on international research projects.

It shares the cost of the project and it allows scientists to share knowledge and expertise.

Now try this

target D-C

1. Name the type of field that is used in cyclotron particle accelerators. **(1 mark)**

target B-A
HIGHER

2. (a) Explain why substances that decay in a short period of time are used as tracers in PET scanners. **(2 marks)**

(b) Explain why the tracer isotopes are made close to where they will be used. **(2 marks)**

Collisions

Momentum and kinetic energy

A moving object has both momentum and kinetic energy (KE).

Momentum = mass × velocity

$$p = mv$$

Kinetic energy = $\frac{1}{2}$ mass × velocity^2

$$KE = \frac{1}{2}mv^2$$

In an elastic collision the kinetic energy of the skaters is the same before and after the collision. Momentum is also conserved.

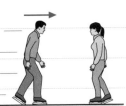 

In an inelastic collision the kinetic energy of the skaters is greater before the collision and less after the collision. Most of the collisions we see in real life are inelastic. But in an inelastic collision the momentum is still conserved.

You need to be able to analyse collisions that take place in one dimension. These are collisions that take place between objects travelling along the same straight line, like railway trucks on a straight piece of track.

Worked example

Fred drops a ball onto a hard surface and it bounces.

(a) Explain how Fred can tell that the collision with the ground is not perfectly elastic.

(b) Since the ball strikes the ground travelling downwards and rebounds travelling upwards it has experienced a change in its momentum. Explain how momentum is conserved in this case.

(a) The ball will not rebound to the same height that it was dropped from so it has lost gravitational potential energy (GPE). At the point of striking the ground all of the GPE has been turned into kinetic energy (KE). If it rebounded with the same KE it would bounce back to the original height, but some of the KE is converted to heat and sound during the collision with the ground.

(b) When the ball hits the ground it exerts a force on the Earth. As a result the Earth accelerates away from the ball. The change in momentum of the ball is exactly balanced by the Earth experiencing an equal but opposite change in momentum. The mass of the Earth is huge compared with that of the ball, so the change in the velocity of the Earth is far too small to detect.

Now try this

1. (a) State the name of the type of collision in which kinetic energy is conserved. **(1 mark)**

(b) In what type(s) of collision is momentum conserved?

(1 mark)

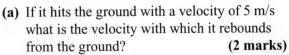

2. A ball makes an elastic collision with the ground.

(a) If it hits the ground with a velocity of 5 m/s what is the velocity with which it rebounds from the ground? **(2 marks)**

(b) Has the momentum of the ball changed during the collision? Explain your answer.

(3 marks)

Calculations in collisions

HIGHER This whole page covers Higher material.

Momentum conservation calculations

> **Worked example**

Before collision

wagon of mass *m* and velocity *u* collides
with a stationary object of mass *M*

After collision

the wagons hook up and move together,
mass (*m* + *M*), with a velocity *v*

A model railway wagon of mass 1 kg travelling at 12 m/s
runs into a second stationary wagon of mass 3 kg.
After the collision the wagons stay linked together and
move together.

Calculate the velocity of the two wagons after the collision.

Momentum = mass × velocity:

$1\,kg \times 12\,m/s = (1 + 3)\,kg \times v$

$v = 12\,kg\,m/s\, /\, 4\,kg$

$v = 3\,m/s$

> If the trucks rebounded and one moved
> in the opposite direction its momentum
> would be negative. Remember
> momentum is always conserved.

> The wagon with larger mass is stationary
> before the collision so has no momentum. The
> wagons move together after the collision with
> a combined mass of (M + m).

Kinetic energy calculations

> **Worked example**

> KE is not a vector quantity. Moving objects have
> positive KE whatever the direction of travel.

(a) Look at the information given in the example above. Calculate the KE before and after the collision.

(a) KE = $\frac{1}{2}$ mass × velocity²

Before the collision the KE of the moving wagon = $\frac{1}{2} \times 1\,kg \times 12^2\,(m/s)^2 = 72\,J$.

After the collision the combined mass is 4 kg and the wagons are moving at 3 m/s,

so the KE = $\frac{1}{2} \times 4\,kg \times 3^2\,(m/s)^2 = 18\,J$.

(b) Explain whether the collision is elastic or inelastic.

(b) KE is **not** conserved therefore the collision is inelastic.

> **Now try this**

target
D-C

1. A car of mass 850 kg is travelling in a straight line at 30 m/s. Calculate its momentum. **(2 marks)**

target
B-A*

2. An air gun pellet with a mass of 1 g is fired into a block of Plasticine on a stationary air
track glider. The mass of the glider and Plasticine is 0.999 kg. After the pellet hits the
Plasticine the glider and Plasticine with the pellet move with a velocity of 5 cm/s.
Calculate the initial velocity of the pellet. **(4 marks)**

Electron–positron annihilation

When a positron collides with an electron the particles cancel one another out in a process called mutual annihilation.

Mutual annihilation

Before collision   After mutual annihilation

−e → ← +e

electron   positron

γ

γ gamma photons are produced as a result of the collision

γ

Radiotracers that emit positrons are used when patients are given PET scans. The positrons will collide with electrons in the patient's body. The mutual annihilation produces gamma rays and these are detected by the PET scanner.

Gamma rays are electromagnetic waves with very short wavelengths. They are emitted in bursts or quanta that carry specific amounts of energy; these quanta are called photons.

Conservation of charge and momentum

Conservation of charge: Note that total electric charge before and after collision is zero. This is because the electron has a charge of −1 and the positron a charge of +1 before the collision. This makes zero. After the collision the gamma rays have no charge.

Conservation of momentum: The positron and electron travel at the same speed in opposite directions, so momentum before they collide is zero. When they collide two gamma photons are emitted at 180° to each other. As the two photons are travelling in opposite directions their total momentum is zero.

Conservation of mass energy

Worked example

Einstein showed that mass is equivalent to energy and vice versa. The equation relating mass and energy is:

$E = mc^2$ energy = mass × (speed of light)^2

(a) Explain what happens to the mass of the electron and position in an annihilation reaction:

(b) An electron has a mass of 9.1×10^{-31} kg. Calculate the total amount of energy produced when an electron and a positron undergo mutual annihilation. (Take the speed of light, $c = 3 \times 10^8$ m/s.)

(a) In electron–positron annihilation two particles with mass disappear. All their mass has been converted into its energy equivalent, and this is carried by the gamma photons.

(b) When electron–positron annihilation takes place the total mass converted into energy is the mass of the electron + the mass of the positron, so $2 \times 9.1 \times 10^{-31}$ kg.

Energy produced
$$= (2 \times 9.1 \times 10^{-31} \text{ kg}) \times (3 \times 10^8 \text{ m/s})^2$$
Answer: 1.64×10^{-13} J

Now try this

target D–C

1. **(a)** State the name of the antimatter particle equivalent to an electron. **(1 mark)**

    (b) State how this particle is different from an electron? **(1 mark)**

target B–A

2. State what three physical properties must be conserved in electron–positron annihilation. **(3 marks)**

HIGHER

Kinetic theory

All substances are found as solids, liquids or gases. These are the three states of matter.

The three states of matter

solid

liquid

gas

In a solid the particles vibrate but they cannot move freely.

In a liquid the particles can move past each other and move around randomly.

In a gas the particles move around very fast and they move all the time. This is because they have a lot of kinetic energy.

Worked example

Explain gas pressure using kinetic theory.

The particles (atoms or molecules) in a gas are continuously moving in a random way and colliding with the container walls. The force from these collisions produces pressure on the walls. On average the number and force of collisions is the same in all directions, so pressure is the same on all the walls of the container.

Absolute zero

As a gas is cooled the average speed of its particles falls and its volume gets smaller. At $-273°C$ the gas volume shrinks to zero. This temperature is called absolute zero. This is the zero temperature on the Kelvin scale. 0 K is equivalent to $-273°C$.

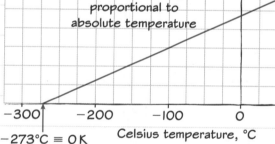

Volume is directly proportional to absolute temperature

Volume, V

-300 -200 -100 0   100

$-273°C \equiv 0K$ Celsius temperature, °C

The temperature of a gas is directly proportional to the average kinetic energy of the gas molecules.

To convert between the Kelvin and Celsius scales use the appropriate formula:

- Celsius → Kelvin ADD 273 to the Celsius temperature
- Kelvin → Celsius SUBTRACT 273 from the Kelvin temperature

Now try this

target D-C

1. (a) Convert 20°C to a temperature on the Kelvin scale.
   (b) Convert 300 K to its equivalent temperature on the Celsius scale. **(2 marks)**

target B-A

2. The temperature of a fixed amount of gas is increased from $-23°C$ to 227°C.
   Explain what happens to the average kinetic energy of the particles in this gas. **(3 marks)**

HIGHER

3. (a) State what happens to the average speed of gas particles as a gas is cooled. **(1 mark)**
   (b) Explain the effect this has on the pressure of the gas in a rigid sealed container. **(2 marks)**

Ideal gas equations 1

Gas at constant pressure

Apparatus like this can be used to investigate what happens to the volume of a gas when the temperature is increased.

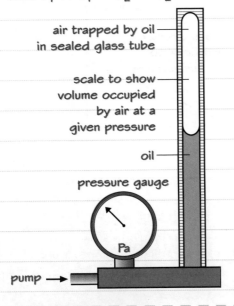

- thermometer
- ruler
- capillary tube open at the top
- concentrated sulfuric acid
- gas being tested (air)
- water

heat

For a fixed amount of gas at constant pressure:

volume is proportional to Kelvin temperature ($V \propto T$)

$$V_1 = \frac{V_2 \times T_1}{T_2}$$

V_1 = volume at the start of the experiment,
V_2 = volume at the end of the experiment,
T_1 = temperature at the start of the experiment and
T_2 = temperature at the end of the experiment.

Temperatures must be in Kelvin, but volumes can be any units providing the same units are used throughout.

Gas at constant temperature

This apparatus can be used to show that $P_1 \times V_1 = P_2 \times V_2$

- air trapped by oil in sealed glass tube
- scale to show volume occupied by air at a given pressure
- oil
- pressure gauge
- Pa
- pump →

Worked example

At atmospheric pressure, 100 kPa, the volume of the column of trapped gas in the apparatus shown on the left is 28 cm³. The pump is used to increase the pressure on the trapped gas to 250 kPa. Calculate the new volume of the trapped air.

Rearrange the equation given on the left to give:

$$V_2 = \frac{V_1 \times P_1}{P_2}$$

where V_1 = 28 cm³, P_1 = 100 kPa and P_2 = 250 kPa

$$V_2 = \frac{28\,cm^3 \times 100\,kPa}{250\,kPa} = 11.2\,cm^3$$

The SI units for P and V are Pa and m³. kPa = 1000 Pascals

The units for pressure and volume do not have to be in SI units, as long as the same units are used throughout.

Now try this

1. Some air is trapped in a syringe by blocking the nozzle of the syringe. The piston in the syringe can move freely in the syringe without leaking any air. Explain what happens if the temperature of the trapped air decreases. **(2 marks)**

HIGHER

2. The pressure in a liquid increases with depth. A bubble of carbon dioxide forms in a glass of fizzy drink. Explain what you would expect to observe, stating any assumptions you have made. **(4 marks)**

Ideal gas equations 2

The general gas equation

$$\frac{P_1 \times V_1}{T_1} = \frac{P_2 \times V_2}{T_2}$$

The value of the constant depends on the amount of gas. This equation assumes that the mass of gas is constant during the changes in P, V and T.

Worked example

A cylinder with a volume of 100 cm³ contains gas at a pressure of 60 atmospheres at −23 °C. When the cylinder is heated to 67 °C its volume expands by 10%. What will the pressure of the gas in the cylinder be at 67 °C?

$P_1 = 60 \, atm$

$T_1 = (-23 + 273) \, K = 250 \, K$, $T_2 = (67 + 273) \, K = 340 \, K$

$V_1 = 100 \, cm^3$, so $V_2 = 1.1 \times 100 \, cm^3 = 110 \, cm^3$

 The pressure is given in atmospheres so the answer will be in atmospheres too.

$$\frac{P_1 \times V_1}{T_1} \qquad \frac{P_2 \times V_2}{T_2}$$

$$P_2 = \frac{P_1 \times V_1 \times T_2}{T_1 \times V_2}$$

 The volume has increased by 10%.

$$P_2 = \frac{60 \, atm \times 100 \, cm^3 \times 340 \, K}{250 \, K \times 110}$$

Answer: the new pressure is 74.2 atm.

 Rearrange the equation to make the new pressure, P_2, the subject.

Bottled gases

In hospitals oxygen and other gases are stored under high pressure in metal bottles or cylinders. This means that the gases take up less room and can be easily stored and transported. When the gas is released from a cylinder its pressure will fall to atmospheric pressure and it will expand to a much larger volume. The new volume can be calculated using the combined gas equation.

Now try this

target
C-B
HIGHER

1. Aerosol deodorant sprays often use gas under high pressure above the deodorant. Why is it unwise to leave them in direct sunlight? **(2 marks)**

target
A-A*
HIGHER

2. An amount of air is trapped inside a cylinder by a piston that can move freely up and down in the cylinder. When the temperature is 17 °C, the volume of the air is 100 cm³ with no weights pressing down on the piston.

(a) A 50 N weight is now added to the piston, causing the volume occupied by the gas to be halved. Explain how the pressure of the trapped air changes. **(2 marks)**

(b) The weight is reduced to 25 N and the temperature of the air is reduced to −3 °C. Calculate the new volume occupied by the gas. **(4 marks)**

Physics extended writing 4

High-energy gamma rays are produced when an electron and a positron annihilate one another as shown by the equation below:

$$e^+ + e^- \rightarrow 2\gamma$$

Explain what the process of annihilation is and what is conserved during the process of annihilation. You may draw a diagram to help you to explain your answer. **(6 marks)**

Sample answer 1

Annihilation is when particles collide and destroy one another, such as when an electron and positron meet each other in space. Mass is not conserved here because there is mass before the collision but none afterwards. Energy is conserved.

This is a basic answer. The explanation of annihilation here is partially correct, although the explanation of conservation of mass-energy is wrong. Charge and momentum could be mentioned as other quantities that are conserved.

Sample answer 2

Annihilation occurs when matter and antimatter collide, resulting in the matter and antimatter destroying one another and gamma rays being released. During the process of annihilation, momentum, charge and total mass-energy are conserved. Charge is conserved here because the total charge before and after the collision is equal to zero. Momentum before and after the collision is also zero, because the electron and positron have equal mass and are travelling towards each other at the same speed. During annihilation, the mass of the electron and positron is converted into energy using the formula $E = mc^2$ where c is the speed of light. After the collision, two gamma photons, moving in opposite directions, are released as shown in the diagram. Although the total mass-energy must be conserved in any reaction, the kinetic energy before and after the collision do not need to be equal.

Before collision

$-e \rightarrow$ ← $+e$

electron   positron

After mutual annihilation

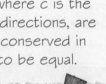

γ gamma photons are produced as a result of the collision

This is an excellent answer. The explanation of annihilation is correct and a full list of quantities that are conserved is also given. The explanation of conservation of momentum is correct. A suitable diagram has also been provided to help support the answer.

1. A radioisotope or tracer can be injected into the body on a biologically active molecule and used to detect whether a patient has a disease such as cancer. Explain how this is done, using the PET scanner as an example. **(6 marks)**

Physics extended writing 5

Worked example

A gas is contained in a cylinder. It is then compressed, very quickly. Use the values on the diagram to calculate the temperature of the gas after it has been compressed.

Explain what happens to the temperature and speed of the gas particles once the gas has been compressed. You should include a calculation in your answer. **(6 marks)**

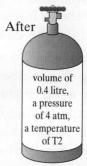

Before — volume of 1 litre, a pressure of 4 atm, a temperature of 400 K

After — volume of 0.4 litre, a pressure of 4 atm, a temperature of T2

Sample answer 1

When a gas is compressed the particles get squashed together which means they move around faster and bump into each other more. They collide with the sides of the container meaning that the gas gets hotter and the particles get faster.

This is a basic answer. It does not contain enough detail to gain high marks. It doesn't explain the relationship between pressure, volume and temperature for a gas, and there is no calculation. The answer does not explain how the speed of the particles in a gas would be affected by compression.

Sample answer 2

$P_1 = 4$ atm $V_1 = 1$ litre $T_1 = 400$ K $P_2 = 20$ atm $V_2 = 0.4$ litre $T_2 = ?$

$$\frac{P_1 \times V_1}{T_1} = \frac{P_2 \times V_2}{T_2} \quad \text{so} \quad T_2 = \frac{P_2 \times V_2 \times T_1}{P_1 \times V_1}$$

$$T_2 = \frac{20 \text{ atm} \times 0.4 \text{ l} \times 400 \text{ K}}{4 \text{ atm} \times 1 \text{ l}} = 800 \text{ K}$$

This is the new temperature of the gas inside the cylinder and it is twice the temperature of the gas before it was compressed. Temperature is directly related to the average kinetic energy of the gas molecules, so if the temperature goes up then the particles must have more kinetic energy. The kinetic energy of the gas depends on the mass of the gas and the speed or velocity of the gas molecules. As the mass of the gas has not changed, the increase in kinetic energy means that the speed of the particles must have increased. The reason for this increase in temperature, speed and kinetic energy is the fact that work has been done on the gas. By compressing the gas quickly, we are doing work on the gas, causing the internal energy of the gas to become greater. This greater internal energy manifests itself as an increase in temperature of the gas.

This is a very detailed answer. It includes a calculation, and explains the results of the calculation in terms of the relationship between temperature, kinetic energy and speed of the gas particles. It also refers to the fact that work has been done on the gas, so it includes the key concept of energy and how it affects the temperature, kinetic energy and speed of the particles present in the gas. The explanation is detailed and correct scientific terms are used.

Now try this   HIGHER

1. Explain the differences between the Celsius and Kelvin scales of temperature and what is meant by the term absolute zero of temperature. **(6 marks)**

Practical work

The Edexcel course includes suggestions for many different investigations. By the time you sit your exams you will have completed a Controlled Assessment, based on one or more of these investigations. But you could also be asked questions about any of these practicals in the exam.

This revision guide includes a brief summary of a method that could be used for each of the suggested investigations. The worked examples below should help with other kinds of questions.

Questions based on practical work could include:
- providing a hypothesis, and justifying it
- writing a method for an investigation
- explaining how to control variables
- drawing a graph to show some results
- writing a conclusion based on results given in the exam paper
- evaluating a method or a conclusion.

Hypotheses and methods

Worked example

A student is investigating the relationship between potential difference, current and resistance. Write a hypothesis and method for this investigation.

Hypothesis: If the resistance in a circuit is increased, the current will be smaller for a particular potential difference. This is because a higher resistance means it is harder for a current to flow through the component.

This is a good hypothesis, because it shows that the student has recalled what they have learned about current, potential difference and resistance.

Method: Set up a circuit with an ammeter in series with a resistor, and with a power pack or battery to provide a constant potential difference. Measure the current. Add another resistor to the circuit and measure the current again. Keep doing this until the current has been measured for 5 different resistances of the circuit.

You should usually have at least 5 data points if you want to draw a graph of your results.

Plot a graph of resistance against current to see the relationship between the two variables.

You must describe a method in the correct order. It may help to jot down some ideas in a blank space on your exam paper to help you to get your ideas in order. If the question asks you to explain the method, remember to say why each step is needed.

Other questions on planning

Other questions on the planning part of a practical could include asking you to:
- explain the apparatus needed
- identify the variables to be controlled and explain how they can be controlled
- identify risks and describe how to manage them.

Practical work

Dealing with evidence

Worked example

The graph shows the results of an investigation to find out how the rate of anaerobic respiration in yeast depends on the concentration of glucose. The rate of respiration was measured by finding the volume of carbon dioxide produced in 10 minutes. Complete the graph by drawing a line of best fit.

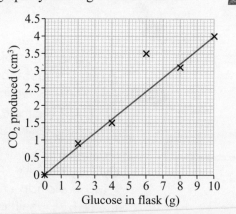

Glucose in flask (g)

A line of best fit can be a straight line or it can be a smooth curve. In this question, the points are along a straight line (apart from the one that obviously does not fit the pattern), so draw a straight line using a ruler.

This is a good answer because the student has drawn a single straight line through most of the points. You will not get any marks for a graph question if you join each of the points using straight lines. Try to include as many points as possible on your line or curve, but ignore any that are obviously not following the pattern of most of your results.

A result that does not fit the pattern is an **anomalous result**. The student has probably made a mistake when measuring or recording the result for 6 g of glucose.

Do not include anomalous results when you are working out means, or when you are drawing lines or curves of best fit.

Conclusions and evaluations

Worked example

A student investigating respiration in yeast had the following hypothesis: 'The rate of respiration will increase when the concentration of glucose increases.'

Look at the graph of their results (above).

(a) Write a conclusion for this investigation.

(a) The graph shows that the rate of respiration of the yeast increases when the concentration of glucose increases. The hypothesis was correct.

This would be a better answer if the conclusion described the shape of the graph in more detail. The graph is a straight line through the origin (0, 0), so the volume of CO_2 produced is proportional to the mass of glucose used. Proportional means that the CO_2 doubles if the glucose doubles.

(b) Evaluate the quality of the conclusion.

(b) All the points except one are close to the line of best fit. The result for 6 g of glucose was probably a mistake. The quality of the data could be improved by using several flasks with each mass of glucose and finding means (averages) of the results.

The conclusion may not apply if more glucose is used. Too much glucose might be bad for the yeast.

Many relationships are only true up to certain values of one of the variables. So you can only really say that your conclusion is valid for the range of the variables you have tested.

Final comments

Here are some other things to remember in your exam.

Read the question carefully. Underline important words in the question to help you to understand what you need to do. Using correct science is great, but no use if it does not actually answer the question!

Use the correct scientific words for things and don't be vague in your answers. For example, saying 'fossil fuels cause pollution' isn't specific enough. Saying *how* they cause pollution is better ('burning fossil fuels causes pollution because carbon dioxide and sulfur dioxide get into the air').

Know what the command words mean at the start of a question. If you are asked to 'explain' then you need to say what happens and how or why it happens. If a question asks you to 'compare' then you need to write down something about all the things you are comparing and how they are similar and different.

Don't use a formula for chemical substances unless the question asks for it. For example, if your answer is carbon dioxide and you write C_2O by mistake (because carbon dioxide is CO_2), it won't be possible to tell that you knew the right answer.

Learn how to balance chemical equations. And remember that all the gases that take part in the reactions you need to know about for this course are diatomic (their formulae are: O_2, Cl_2, N_2, and so on).

Revise the investigations you have carried out during the course. You may be asked questions on practical work in the exam.

Show your working for calculation questions, even if you use a calculator. And don't forget to include the units with your final answer.

Write your name here
Surname   Other names

Edexcel GCSE

Centre Number   Candidate Number

Physics
Unit P3: Applications of Physics

Higher Tier

Time: 1 hour   Paper Reference
                               XXX

You must have: Total Marks
Calculator, ruler

Instructions
- Use **black** ink or ball-point pen.
- **Fill in the boxes** at the top of this page with your name, centre number and candidate number.
- Answer **all** questions.
- Answer the questions in the spaces provided – there may be more space than you need.

Information
- The total mark for this paper is 60.
- The marks for **each** question are shown in brackets – use this as a guide as to how much time to spend on each question.
- Questions labelled with an **asterisk (*)** are ones where the quality of your written communication will be assessed – you should take particular care with your spelling, punctuation and grammar, as well as the clarity of expression, on these questions.

Advice
- Read each question carefully before you start to answer it.
- Keep an eye on the time.
- Try to answer every question.
- Check your answers if you have time at the end.

Turn over ▶

P40176A
edexcel
advancing learning, changing lives

Using formula triangles

There will be a formula sheet in the exam, so you do not need to memorise equations, but you do need to be able to rearrange them.

If you cannot remember how to do this, you need to memorise the formula triangles given with formulae in this book. For example, $P = I \times V$ will be given in the exam paper. If you need to work out the voltage (V), cover up the V on the formula triangle. This will tell you that you need to divide P by I to get your answer.

$P = I \times V$ (given in exam)

This can be rearranged as:

$V = \dfrac{P}{I}$ or $I = \dfrac{P}{V}$

100

Periodic table

You will be given a copy of the periodic table in your exam. It will look something like this.

Key

| relative atomic mass |
| atomic symbol |
| name |
| atomic (proton) number |

| 1 | H | hydrogen | 1 |

1	2												3	4	5	6	7	0
																		4 **He** helium 2
7 **Li** lithium 3	9 **Be** beryllium 4												11 **B** boron 5	12 **C** carbon 6	14 **N** nitrogen 7	16 **O** oxygen 8	19 **F** fluorine 9	20 **Ne** neon 10
23 **Na** sodium 11	24 **Mg** magnesium 12												27 **Al** aluminium 13	28 **Si** silicon 14	31 **P** phosphorus 15	32 **S** sulfur 16	35.5 **Cl** chlorine 17	40 **Ar** argon 18
39 **K** potassium 19	40 **Ca** calcium 20	45 **Sc** scandium 21	48 **Ti** titanium 22	51 **V** vanadium 23	52 **Cr** chromium 24	55 **Mn** manganese 25	56 **Fe** iron 26	59 **Co** cobalt 27	59 **Ni** nickel 28	63.5 **Cu** copper 29	65 **Zn** zinc 30		70 **Ga** gallium 31	73 **Ge** germanium 32	75 **As** arsenic 33	79 **Se** selenium 34	80 **Br** bromine 35	84 **Kr** krypton 36
85 **Rb** rubidium 37	88 **Sr** strontium 38	89 **Y** yttrium 39	91 **Zr** zirconium 40	93 **Nb** niobium 41	96 **Mo** molybdenum 42	[98] **Tc** technetium 43	101 **Ru** ruthenium 44	103 **Rh** rhodium 45	106 **Pd** palladium 46	108 **Ag** silver 47	112 **Cd** cadmium 48		115 **In** indium 49	119 **Sn** tin 50	122 **Sb** antimony 51	128 **Te** tellurium 52	127 **I** iodine 53	131 **Xe** xenon 54
133 **Cs** caesium 55	137 **Ba** barium 56	139 **La*** lanthanum 57	178 **Hf** hafnium 72	181 **Ta** tantalum 73	184 **W** tungsten 74	186 **Re** rhenium 75	190 **Os** osmium 76	192 **Ir** iridium 77	195 **Pt** platinum 78	197 **Au** gold 79	201 **Hg** mercury 80		204 **Tl** thallium 81	207 **Pb** lead 82	209 **Bi** bismuth 83	[209] **Po** polonium 84	[210] **At** astatine 85	[222] **Rn** radon 86
[223] **Mn** francium 87	[226] **Ra** radium 88	[227] **Ac*** actinium 89	[261] **Rf** rutherfordium 104	[262] **Db** dubnium 105	[266] **Sg** seaborgium 106	[264] **Bh** bohrium 107	[277] **Hs** hassium 108	[268] **Mt** meitnerium 109	[271] **Ds** darmstadtium 110	[272] **Rg** roentgenium 111								

Elements with atomic numbers 112-116 have been reported but not fully authenicated

* The lanthanoids (atomic numbers 58-71) and the actinoids (atomic numbers 90-103) have been omitted.

The relevant atomic masses of copper and chlorine have not been rounded to the nearest whole number.

Answers

You will find some advice next to some of the answers. This is written in italics. It is not part of the mark scheme but just gives you a little more information.

Biology answers

1. Rhythms

1. Photoperiodicity is a change in response to changing day length; **(1)** a circadian rhythm is a response or behaviour that changes on a cycle of about 24 hours. **(1)**

2. Plants that germinate in spring **(1)** will get the light and warmth they need for growth and reproduction over the summer. **(1)**

3. When the person was in Mexico, their biological clock would set a sleep pattern that matches the time of night there; **(1)** when they arrive in the UK, night-time is at a different time, so they would not feel sleepy until it is the time that would be nightfall in Mexico/they would feel jet-lagged; **(1)** this is because sleep is a circadian rhythm. **(1)**

2. Plant defences

1. symptom **(1)** because it is what you feel or show as a result of an infection or disorder. **(1)**

2. Pests and pathogens damage plants; **(1)** if the plant produces chemicals that protect it against attack, then the plants will be able to produce more food and so grow more rapidly. **(1)**

3. Using chemicals to kill pathogens and pests reduces damage to the plants; **(1)** so the crops give a greater yield; **(1)** the farmer will get more money for the larger yield. **(1)**

3. Growing microorganisms

1. Aseptic techniques kill microorganisms; **(1)** this prevents microorganisms from causing infections. **(1)**

2. Pasteurisation heats the food briefly **(1)** because this kills the microorganisms; **(1)** without the microorganisms, the food stays fresh. **(1)**

3. Pasteur's experiment showed that only the broth that the microbes could get to from the air went off/bad; **(1)** so microbes/microorganisms cannot just suddenly appear; **(1)** 'aseptic technique' means that once microbes are killed no more will arise unless they come into contact with something that contains microbes/is not sterile. **(1)**

4. Vaccines

1. A vaccine contains a dead or harmless form of a pathogen or antigenic material that is used to immunise a person. **(1)** Immunisation means giving a vaccine to cause an immune response in the body. **(1)**

2. (a) Memory lymphocytes that recognise the antigens of the pathogen remain in the blood after the first response has gone; **(1)** the memory lymphocytes respond to any later infection by the pathogen. **(1)**
   (b) The antibodies and memory lymphocytes only recognise the antigens of that pathogen; **(1)** different pathogens have different antigens. **(1)**

3. Any two from: Infection can only be transmitted from an infected individual to an uninfected individual; vaccinated people are immune and so cannot become infected; if most people are immune, the chances of an unvaccinated person meeting an infected person are very small. **(2)**

5. Antibodies

1. Monoclonal antibodies can be targeted better than radiotherapy; **(1)** because they are specific for certain cells; **(1)** this means that other cells are not affected as they can be in radiotherapy. **(1)**

2. The secondary response is (much) larger than the primary response; **(1)** the secondary response is (much) faster than the primary response. **(1)**

3. Normally cells that produce antibodies don't divide, so you can't get large numbers of cells that produce the same antibodies; **(1)** cancer cells do divide but cannot produce antibodies; **(1)** a fusion of the two cells produces hybridoma cells that make the antibodies and that can divide to make more cells that produce the same antibodies. **(1)**

6. The kidneys

1. (a) urea **(1)**
   (b) liver **(1)**

2. kidney, ureter, bladder, urethra (**2 marks** for all in correct order, **1 mark** for any three in correct order)

3. Body processes make waste products including urea; **(1)** if too much urea builds up in the blood, it becomes toxic, which will damage the body. **(1)**

7. Inside the kidneys

1. They filter small molecules out of the blood into the nephron. **(1)**

2. (a) the reabsorption of some molecules but not others from the nephron **(1)**
   (b) regulating the water content of the blood **(1)**

3. Both urea and glucose are filtered from the blood into the nephron in the glomerulus and Bowman's capsule; **(1)** glucose is selectively reabsorbed back into the blood from the convoluted tubule of the nephron, but urea is not; **(1)** this leaves urea in the urine but removes all the glucose. **(1)**

8. The role of ADH

1. produced in the pituitary gland **(1)** and acts on the kidneys **(1)**

2. after exercise **(1)** because water will have been lost from the body in sweat during exercise **(1)** and more ADH is secreted by the pituitary gland when blood water content is low **(1)**

3. Negative feedback mechanisms help to restore 'normal' levels of controlled factors (such as blood water content) after changes; **(1)** so negative feedback mechanisms help maintain a constant internal environment. **(1)**

9. The menstrual cycle

1. (a) around day 14 **(1)**
   (b) from day 1, usually for between 4 and 7 days **(1)**
   (c) from the end of menstruation to day 28 **(1)**

2. If the egg is fertilised, the uterus lining is maintained. **(1)**

10. Hormone control

1. (a) in the ovaries **(1)**
   (b) in the pituitary gland **(1)**

2. fall in oestrogen and progesterone levels **(1)**

3. (a) thickening of uterus wall and triggering of LH release **(1)**
   (b) thickening of uterus wall **(1)**
   (c) stimulates growth and development of egg in ovary **(1)**
   (d) triggers ovulation **(1)**

11. Fertilisation

1. Infertility is the inability to have children; **(1)** any two from: it can be treated by IVF; egg donation; using a surrogate mother; hormones (**1 mark** for each to max. of **2**)

2. The tail makes it possible for the sperm to swim **(1)** and the mitochondria in the middle section of the tail supply the energy from respiration to make the tail move. **(1)**

3. The cell membrane of the egg changes when the first sperm enters **(1)** and this prevents entry by any other sperm. **(1)**

12. Sex determination

1. at fertilisation **(1)**, as that is when the two gametes fuse to produce a cell with two sex chromosomes **(1)**

2. chance is 50%; **(1)** diagram or Punnett square as shown on page 14 (**1** mark for parent phenotype, **1** for gametes, **1** for possible outcomes)

3. There is always an X from the mother **(1)** because women are all XX and will only pass on an X chromsome. **(1)**

13. Sex-linked inheritance

1. A sex-linked disorder is carried on a gene on the part of the X chromosome that is not matched by the Y chromosome; **(1)** men are more likely to have a sex-linked condition than women because men only have one X chromosome. **(1)**

2. **(a)** Using suitable notation for the chromosomes and alleles, such as X^R for normal vision and X^r for colour blindness, and X for Y chromosomes, **(1)** a genetic diagram or Punnett square correctly set out like this:

		gametes from mother	
		X^R	X^r
gametes from father	X^R	$X^R X^R$	$X^R X^r$
	Y	$X^R Y$	$X^r Y$

(**1** mark for correct gametes, **1** mark for correct genotypes of offspring)
  (b) (i) daughter 0% **(1)**
       (ii) son 50% **(1)**

14 and 15. Biology extended writing 1 and 2

Answers can be found on page 108.

16. Courtship

1. a behaviour that is carried out to attract a mate **(1)** and advertises the individual's reproductive quality **(1)**

2. Advantage – any one from: the bond between the pair means they look after each other/young; once a good partner has been chosen, they are 'kept' **(1)**
   Disadvantage – if one partner dies the other must find another mate **(1)**

3. The best tail display shows which male is strongest/healthiest **(1)** so offspring will inherit genes from the male for strength/health **(1)** and the female's genes are more likely to be in a strong/healthy individual and passed on to future generations. **(1)**

17. Parenting

1. behaviour where a parent looks after the young **(1)**

2. Any two examples, such as: feeds a young baby, keeps it warm, teaches a child new skills. **(2)**

3. **(a)** It gives them protection from predators and other dangerous situations/helps them learn survival skills e.g. hunting **(1)** and so increases their chance of survival to adulthood. **(1)**
   (b) Advantage – it increases the chance of her genes being passed on to future generations **(1)**
   Disadvantage – any suitable answer, such as: she has to hunt for more food for the young as well herself; she may have to take risks to protect her young from predators. **(1)**

18. Simple behaviours

1. It is not a learned response. **(1)**

2. The gosling has learned to identify the object as 'mother'; **(1)** this learning cannot be changed later. **(1)**

3. If the chicks follow the mother as a result of imprinting they will get parental care/have protection and be shown where to find food; **(1)** this will increase their chance of survival and passing on the genes for imprinting to the next generation. **(1)**

19. Learned behaviour

1. habituation **(1)**

2. Operant conditioning is when a chance behaviour becomes more common because it is rewarded; **(1)** classical conditioning is when a second stimulus becomes associated with the normal stimulus and eventually can produce the response without the normal stimulus. **(1)**

3. This is operant conditioning **(1)** because the rat found its way to the food the first time by chance but the reward of food makes it head more directly to that spot the next time. **(1)**

20. Animal communication

1. It increases the chances of survival for the individuals of the group. **(1)**

2. Any two suitable examples, such as: sound signals (e.g. shouting to warn or frighten), chemical signals (e.g. pheromones to attract members of the opposite sex), visual signals (e.g. waving arms to attract attention, body posture to show strength or fear, facial expression showing surprise or happiness) **(2)**

3. Any two suitable but different answers, e.g. to frighten off lions; to protect weaker/young elephants in the group; so that they have a 360° field of view; to make it more difficult for lions to get close enough to an individual to attack it/so that they cannot be attacked from the rear. **(2)**

21. Plant communication

1. Any two suitable and different examples, such as: communicate with pollinating animals using scent, communicate with other plants by chemicals in the ground or in the air. **(2)**

2. Where a change in one species causes a change in a different species. **(1)**

3. Flowers that smell more like rotting flesh will attract more carrion flies; **(1)** so flowers that smell are more likely to receive pollen from flies that have just been to flowers of the same plant species; **(1)** this increases the chance of the plant's egg cells being fertilised and so passing its genes for smelly flowers on to the next generation. **(1)**

22. Human evolution

1. fossils **(1)** stone tools **(1)**

2. Any two suitable features, such as: increase in brain size, increase in height, upright posture and ability to walk over long distances. **(2)**

3. An increase in the complexity of the way the tools are made and in the range of tools produced **(1)** suggests that humans were developing in intelligence/skill OR suggests that humans developed their skills of tool-making as the skills were passed from generation to generation. **(1)**

23. Human migration

1. Sea levels were much lower due to the Ice Age; **(1)** so they may have been able to swim or walk across where there is water now. **(1)**

2. Mitochondria in the sperm do not enter the egg **(1)** during fertilisation. **(1)**

3. The mitochondrial DNA is easier to extract **(1)** and less likely to degrade over time. **(1)**

24. Biology extended writing 3

Answers can be found on page 108.

25. Biotechnology

1. It is a molecule that is made by a living organism. **(1)**

2. To keep the fermenter at the right temperature and pH (optimum conditions) **(1)** because conditions will change as the microorganism grows, e.g. using up nutrients; **(1)** if conditions change inside the fermenter then growth of microorganisms (and so production of biomolecules) will slow down. **(1)**

3. If it wasn't stirred the cells would settle to the bottom as a result of gravity; **(1)** if the cells are clumped, those in the middle of a clump can't get the nutrients/oxygen that they need for growing rapidly; **(1)** so the rate of production of biomolecules will slow down. **(1)**

26. Microorganisms for food

1. Any two suitable answers, such as: bread, cheese, yogurt, beer, wine, mycoprotein. **(2)**

2. Microorganisms can be grown in fermenters or other vessels where the conditions are controlled; **(1)** as long as the fermenters/vessels can be set up and run properly, they can produce microorganisms almost anywhere. **(1)**

3. Waste products from other processes can be used as nutrients for the microorganisms; **(1)** this means the waste products do not need to be disposed of in the environment, which could use land or cause pollution. **(1)**

27. Mycoprotein

1. a food made using the *Fusarium* fungus **(1)**

2. Red meat contains saturated fat, which is a risk factor for heart disease; **(1)** mycoprotein contains no saturated fat and so will reduce the risk of heart disease. **(1)**

3. *Fusarium* sp. fungus is added to a broth containing glucose syrup and minerals in a fermenter; **(1)** ammonia and air are bubbled through the broth to supply nitrogen and oxygen to the fungal hyphae; **(1)** conditions in the fermenter are controlled by venting excess gases produced by the fungus and by removing excess heat by a cooling system; **(1)** fungus is extracted from the broth, heat-treated to remove the bitter taste, then dried and pressed to form mycoprotein. **(1)**

28. Enzyme technology

1. (a) trap the enzyme in an alginate bead **(1)**
   (b) The beads are easier to separate from the product so that the enzyme can be used again. **(1)**

2. The enzyme will break down the sucrose to glucose and fructose, **(1)** which will produce a sweet, soft centre to the chocolate. **(1)**

3. Any two suitable answers, such as: it will be easier to make lots more enzyme this way than extracting it from calves' stomachs; many people object to calves being killed; this makes cheese that is suitable for vegetarians. **(2)**

29. DNA technology

1. making genetically modified organisms **(1)**

2. human gene cut out of human DNA using restriction enzymes that leave sticky ends on the gene; **(1)** plasmid removed from bacterium and cut open using same restriction enzymes that produce matching sticky ends; **(1)** human gene and plasmid mixed with DNA ligase enzyme that joins the sticky ends together to make recombinant plasmid; **(1)** recombinant plasmid inserted into another bacterium where it makes the human insulin **(1)**

3. The bacteria can be grown in ideal conditions in large fermenters **(1)** so that they produce large quantities of insulin quickly and cheaply. **(1)**

30. Global food security

1. Human population is increasing, **(1)** and so more food will be needed to feed everyone properly. **(1)**

2. Biofuel crops need space to grow in, which can take land needed for growing food crops; **(1)** if less food is grown, then there might not be enough for everyone to eat, which reduces global food security. **(1)**

3. Plant breeding programmes produce higher-yielding varieties of wheat plants; **(1)** pest management strategies decrease the amount of damage to crops by pests and so increase the yield from each plant. **(1)** *'Planting a greater area of crop' is not a suitable answer, because the question has asked for increased yield – the amount of wheat produced in a given area.*

31. A GM future?

1. (a) Any one suitable example, such as: purple tomato, golden rice, herbicide-resistant wheat. **(1)**
   (b) Any one from: genetic modification can add a gene that isn't normally found in the species, but selective breeding only uses genes that are in the species; genetic modification is much faster than selective breeding to produce the required characteristic. **(1)**

2. If people who have a diet deficient in vitamin A eat golden rice, they are less likely to suffer blindness; **(1)** but people who have a diet deficient in vitamin A may be poor people who cannot afford to buy the golden rice. **(1)**

3. Experiments have shown that mice with cancer live longer if they eat flavonoids; **(1)** this suggests that people with cancer might live longer if they eat flavonoids; **(1)** flavonoids are not normally found in tomatoes so producing transgenic tomatoes that make flavonoids will make it easier for people to eat flavonoids. **(1)**

32. Insect-resistant plants

1. Seed for the transgenic plants costs more than seed for non-transgenic plants so farmers are less likely to be able to afford it. **(1)**

2. gene for Bt toxin cut out of *Bacillus thuringiensis* bacterium; **(1)** gene inserted into plasmid from *Agrobacterium tumefaciens*; **(1)** plasmid inserted into another *A. tumefaciens*; **(1)** bacterium infects cells in leaf discs from wheat plant; **(1)** sections of the leaf discs are used to grow whole plants in which all cells have the gene for Bt toxin **(1)**

3. Any three from: insect-resistant plants kill only the insects that eat them and not other insects; **(1)** chemical insecticides often kill many species of insect, not just the pest species; **(1)** so there will be fewer predators of insects, such as birds like robins; **(1)** therefore chemical insecticides are more likely to damage food webs, such as reducing the number of birds that eat insects, and could reduce the numbers of predators that feed on the birds, etc. **(1)** *For the last mark, you should give some detail of how the food web may be damaged.*

33 and 34. Biology extended writing 4 and 5

Answers can be found on page 108.

Chemistry answers

35. Water testing

1. Qualitative analysis looks at the types of substances in a sample; **(1)** quantitative analysis looks at how much of a substance there is in a sample. **(1)**

2. (a) Put some of the sample into the flame (on a damp wooden splint); **(1)** a green-blue flame should be seen if copper(II) ions are present. **(1)**
   (b) Dissolve some of the sample in water and add a few drops of sodium hydroxide solution; **(1)** a pale blue precipitate should be seen if copper(II) ions are present. **(1)**

3. Add sodium hydroxide solution to produce a white precipitate; **(1)** only the sample containing aluminium ions will redissolve when excess sodium hydroxide is added. **(1)**

36. Safe water

1. Add sodium hydroxide and warm the mixture; **(1)** damp red litmus should turn blue if ammonium ions were present; **(1)** in another sample, add a few drops of nitric acid, then add a few drops of silver nitrate solution; **(1)** a white precipitate should form if chloride ions are present. **(1)**

2. $Ag^+(aq) + I^-(aq) \rightarrow AgI(s)$ (**1** mark for correct formulae, **1** mark for correct state symbols)

37. Safe limits

1. Any two points from: to test blood, to test urine, to help doctors identify illnesses. **(2)**

2. to make sure the water is safe to drink; **(1)** high levels of aluminium in the blood are linked to Alzheimer's disease **(1)**

3. Collect a sample of the water from the stream and add a few drops of sodium hydroxide solution **(1)**; a green precipitate will form if iron(II) irons are present; **(1)** a brown precipitate will form if iron(III) ions are present. **(1)**

38. Water solutes

1. (a) calcium ions **(1)** magnesium ions **(1)**
   (b) $4 \text{ g} \div 2 \text{ dm}^3$ **(1)** $= 2 \text{ g dm}^{-3}$ **(1)**

2. volume $= 500 \div 1000 = 0.5 \text{ dm}^3$; **(1)** concentration $= 0.02 \div 0.5$ **(1)** $= 0.04 \text{ g dm}^{-3}$ **(1)**

39. Hard and soft water

1. (a) calcium hydrogencarbonate **(1)**
   (b) calcium sulfate **(1)** *You could also say magnesium sulfate.*
   (c) Boiling causes calcium hydrogencarbonate to break down, **(1)** producing insoluble calcium carbonate. **(1)**

2. (a) Both type of hardness are caused by calcium/magnesium ions, **(1)** which are removed from the water by ion exchange resins. **(1)**
   (b) Ion exchange resins swap calcium ions for sodium ions; **(1)** sodium chloride replaces calcium ions in the resin with sodium ions; **(1)** sodium ions are used up and must be replaced every few weeks **(1)**.

40. Moles and mass

1. (a) $2 \times 16 = 32$ (1)
   (b) $2 \times 1 + 16 = 18$ (1)
   (c) $(2 \times 12) + (5 \times 1) + 16 + 1 = 24 + 5 + 16 + 1 = 46$ (1)
2. (a) $6 \div 12$ (1) $= 0.5$ mol (1)
   (b) Relative formula mass of hydrogen $= 2 \times 1 = 2$; (1)
   $4 \div 2 = 2$ mol (1)

41. Moles in solution

1. Relative formula mass $= 24 + 16 = 40$; (1)
   mass $= 40 \times 0.25 = 10$ g (1)
2. (a) $200\ cm^3 = 200 \div 1000 = 0.2\ dm^3$; (1) concentration
   $= 0.04 \div 0.2 = 0.2\ mol\ dm^{-3}$ (1)
   (b) Relative formula mass $= 24 + (2 \times (16 +1)) = 58$; (1)
   concentration $= 0.2 \times 58 = 11.6\ g\ dm^{-3}$ (1)

42. Preparing soluble salts 1

1. (a) zinc oxide + hydrochloric acid → zinc chloride + water (1)
   (b) to make sure that all the acid has reacted (1)
2. (a) $ZnO + 2HCl \rightarrow ZnCl_2 + H_2O$ (1 mark for correct formulae, 1 mark for correct balancing)
   (b) Any three points from: add zinc oxide to hydrochloric acid; until no more zinc oxide will react; filter to remove excess zinc oxide; evaporate the water from the solution. (3)

43. Preparing soluble salts 2

1. (a) named single indicator such as phenolphthalein or methyl orange (1)
   (b) results that are close to each other, identical, or within a certain range (1)
2. Any two points from: use a pipette to measure the liquid in the flask; swirl the flask; add solution drop wise near the end-point; wash the inside of the flask with water; repeat until concordant. (2)
3. $H^+(aq) + OH^-(aq) \rightarrow H_2O(l)$ (1 mark for correct formulae, 1 mark for state symbols)

44. Titration calculations

1. (a) $(25.5\ cm^3 + 29.0\ cm^3 +27.5\ cm^3)/3$ (1) $= 27.3\ cm^3$ (1)
   (b) $KOH + HCl \rightarrow KCl + H_2O$ moles of nitric acid $= 28.00 \div 1000 \times 0.20 = 0.0056$ mol; (1) moles of potassium hydroxide must be the same so $= 0.0056$; (1) concentration of potassium hydroxide $= 0.0056 \div 25.00 \times 1000 = 0.224\ mol\ dm^{-3}$ (1)

45. More calculations from equations

1. moles of sodium hydroxide $= 0.20 \times 25.00 \div 1000 = 0.005$ mol; (1) number of moles of hydrochloric acid $= 0.005$ mol; (1) volume of hydrochloric acid $= 0.005 \div 0.5 = 0.01\ dm^3$ (10 cm^3) (1)
2. moles of hydrochloric acid $= 0.25 \times 20.00 \div 1000 = 0.005$ mol; (1) number of moles of sodium hydroxide $= 0.005$ mol; (1) volume of sodium hydroxide $= 0.005 \div 0.10 = 0.05\ dm^3$ (50 cm^3) (1)
3. moles of sodium hydroxide $= 0.10 \times 20.00 \div 1000 = 0.002$ mol; (1) number of moles of sulfuric acid $= 0.002 \div 2 = 0.001$ mol; (1) volume of sulfuric acid $= 0.001 \div 0.25 = 0.004\ dm^3$ (4 cm^3) (1)

46 and 47. Chemistry extended writing 1 and 2

Answers can be found on page 109.

48. Electrolysis

1. (a) Liquid containing ions that can move and carry the current during electrolysis. (1)
   (b) the cathode/negative electrode (1)
2. The ions in copper chloride solution can move around, (1) but they cannot move around in solid copper chloride. (1)
3. Sodium ions move to the cathode/negative electrode (1) and chloride ions move to the anode/positive electrode. (1)

49. Making and using sodium

1. street lamps (1) because it gives out yellow light when an electric current is passed through its vapour (1) OR coolant in a nuclear power station (1) because it has a high heat capacity (1)

2. bubbles of gas forming (1)
3. (a) Cathode: $Na^+(l) + e^- \rightarrow Na(l)$ (1 mark for correct formulae, 1 mark for state symbols); anode: $2Cl^-(l) \rightarrow Cl_2(g) + 2e^-$ (1 mark for correct formulae, 1 mark for correctly balanced)
   (b) The reaction at the cathode is reduction because sodium ions gain electrons; (1) the reaction at the anode is oxidation because the chloride ions lose electrons. (1)

50. Electrolysis of salt water

1. (a) hydrogen at the cathode/negative electrode; (1) chlorine at the anode/positive electrode (1)
   (b) The hydrogen ions and hydroxide ions come from water in the solution. (1)
2. (a) Na^+ and Cl^- ions, (1) H^+ and OH^- ions (1)
   (b) Cathode: $2H^+(aq) + 2e^- \rightarrow H_2(g)$ (1 mark for correct formulae, 1 mark for correctly balanced)
   Anode: $2Cl^-(aq) \rightarrow Cl_2(g) + 2e^-$ (1 mark for correct formulae, 1 mark for correctly balanced)
   (c) The solution contains sodium ions from the sodium chloride (1) and hydroxide ions from the water. (1)

51. More electrolysis

1. (a) brown (copper) metal forming at the cathode; (1) the anode gradually gets smaller (1)
   (b) Anode: silver; (1) cathode: the steel spoon (1)
2. (a) Two points from: copper atoms in the electrode lose electrons; the copper ions go into solution; impurities fall to the bottom. (2)
   (b) The electrolyte must contain copper ions (1) and these are free to move around in solution. (1)
   (c) The sludge contains valuable metals (e.g. silver, gold, platinum), (1) and these can be purified and sold. (1)

52. Gas calculations 1

1. They both contain the same number of molecules (1) because one mole of any gas contains the same number of molecules. (1)
2. $0.1 \times 24 = 2.4\ dm^3$ (1)
3. $120 \div 24\ 000 = 0.005$ mol (1)

53. Gas calculations 2

1. (a) $540 \div 24 = 22.5$ mol (1)
   (b) $2 \times 22.5 = 45$ mol (1) *If you got the answer to part (a) wrong, you would still get this mark if you multiplied that answer by 2 and showed your working.*

54. Fertilisers

1. air (1) natural gas (1)
2. Ammonia breaks down (1) to form nitrogen and hydrogen. (1)
3. It is a reaction that can happen in both directions; (1) in the Haber process, the forward reaction makes ammonia from nitrogen and hydrogen, and the reverse direction makes nitrogen and hydrogen from ammonia. (1)

55. Equilibrium

1. no change; (1) because there are the same number of molecules on each side of the equation (1)
2. (a) It is decreased (1) because there are more molecules of gas on the left-hand side. (1) The equilibrium moves in the direction of the smaller number of molecules when the pressure is increased. (1)
   (b) It is exothermic (1) because more N_2O_4 is formed when the temperature is decreased. (1)

56. The Haber process

1. Catalysts reduce the time taken to reach equilibrium, (1) which means that an acceptable yield is produced in an acceptable time. (1)
2. (a) 25–29% (1)
   (b) (i) Higher pressure gives a higher yield; (1) but high pressures cost a lot of money to maintain. (1)
   (ii) It would give a higher yield; (1) but the rate would be too low. (1)

ANSWERS

57. Chemistry extended writing 3
Answers can be found on page 109.

58. Fermentation and alcohol
1. (a) Use fractional distillation (1) because ethanol has a lower boiling point than water. (1)
   (b) Different drinks have different percentages of ethanol; (1) fractional distillation is used to provide strong drinks/named strong drink such as whisky. (1)
2. Alcohol has harmful effects on health OR people may commit crimes when drunk; (1) increasing the cost may reduce consumption. (1) *There are likely to be many possible answers for a question like this.*

59. Ethanol production
1. Ethanol is heated to a high temperature; (1) in the presence of a catalyst; (1) $C_2H_5OH \rightarrow C_2H_4 + H_2O$. (1)
2. Advantage of using sugar – one from: sugar is a renewable resource; fermentation needs moderate temperatures. (1)

   Disadvantage of using sugar – one from: land may need to be cleared to grow sugar beet; sugar beet cannot be grown everywhere; the product is not pure and has to undergo fractional distillation; which means less land for food production. (1)

   Advantage of using crude oil – one from: the product is pure; the process is fast. (1)

   Disadvantage of using crude oil – one from: crude oil is a non-renewable resource; the process needs high temperatures; crude oil may need to be imported. (1)

60. Homologous series
1. Two of the following: same general formula; gradual variation in physical properties; similar chemical properties. (2)
2. C_4H_{10}; (1)

   (1)
   $$H-\overset{\displaystyle H}{\underset{\displaystyle H}{C}}-\overset{\displaystyle H}{\underset{\displaystyle H}{C}}-\overset{\displaystyle H}{\underset{\displaystyle H}{C}}-\overset{\displaystyle H}{\underset{\displaystyle H}{C}}-H$$
3. temperature between 85°C and 100°C; (1) the boiling point increases as the number of carbon atoms increases/propanol has more carbon atoms than ethanol (1)
4. Three of the following: alkenes have C=C bonds and alkanes do not; alkenes are unsaturated molecules and alkanes are saturated; alkenes decolourise bromine water but alkanes do not; they have a different general formula (OR state two general formula). (3)

61. Ethanoic acid
1. oxidation (1)
2. flavouring; (1) preservative (1)
3. Two from the following: reacts with metals to form salt and hydrogen; reacts with bases to form salts (ethanoates) and water; reacts with carbonates to form salts (ethanoates), water and carbon dioxide; turns universal indicator red/orange. (2)
4. (a) Three from the following: ethanol has six hydrogen atoms but ethanoic acid has four; ethanol has a hydroxyl (–OH) group but ethanoic acid has a carboxyl group (–COOH); ethanol has one oxygen atom but ethanoic acid has two; ethanoic acid has C=O but ethanol does not. (3)
   (b) C_3H_7COOH (1)

62. Esters
1. (a) food flavourings; (1) perfumes (1)
   (b) ethyl ethanoate; (1) water (1)
2. The bottles are shredded and melted to form fibres, (1) which are woven to form fleece for clothing. (1)
3. $CH_3COOH + C_2H_5OH \rightarrow CH_3COOC_2H_5 + H_2O$ (correct reactants, 1 mark; H_2O as the other product, 1 mark)

63. Fats, oils and soap
1. esters (1)
2. Oils and fats are boiled (1) with concentrated alkali solution. (1)
3. (a) The anion has a negatively charged (1) hydrophilic head (1) and a hydrophobic tail. (1)
   (b) The hydrophobic part of the soap anion dissolves in the grease (1) and the hydrophilic part dissolves in the water. (1)
4. Any two from the following: hydrogen is bubbled through the oil; in the presence of a (nickel) catalyst; which removes the C=C unsaturation in a process called catalytic hydrogenation (2)

64 and 65. Chemistry extended writing 4 and 5
Answers can be found on page 109.

Physics answers
66. Radiation in medicine
1. The intensity of the Sun's radiation decreases with distance from the Sun, (1) because it becomes more and more spread out. (1) Calculation of decrease e.g. $1.4/5^2$. (1)
2. (a) Area of panels = 14 m²
   $P = I \times A = 1.4\,kW/m^2 \times 14\,m^2$ (1) $= 19.6\,kW$ or $19\,600\,W$ (1)

67. How eyes work
1. (a) pupil (1)
   (b) iris (1)
2. (a) 25 cm (but allow 20–30 cm) (1)
   (b) The near point is the closest point that a person with normal vision can comfortably focus on. (1)

68. Sight problems
1. (a) A converging lens bends rays passing through it towards the axis and therefore each other. (1)
   (b) A diverging lens bends rays passing through it away from each other. (1)
2. (a) The far point is closer to the eye than normal. (1)
   (b) The near point is further from the eye than normal. (1)

69. Correcting sight problems
1. by wearing glasses (spectacles); (1) by wearing contact lenses (1)
2. (a) It makes the cornea act like a diverging lens. (1)
   (b) short-sighted (1)

70. Different lenses
1. More powerful lenses are more curved (fatter), (1) so the +5D lens is fatter than the +2D lens. (1)
2. rearrange the formula for power: focal length = 1/power; (1) focal length = 1/1; (1) focal length of a +D lens is 1 m (100 cm) (1)

71. The lens equation
1. (a) real (image of the Sun formed on the paper being burned) (1)
   (b) real (1)
   (c) virtual (1)
2. (a) The eye lens will be in its thinnest state, (1) because the rays of light coming from a distant object are nearly parallel; (1) so they do not have to be bent very much to be focused on the retina. (1) *Both the lens and the cornea refract the light but for this question we can assume that the eye has a lens 25 mm away from the retina.*
   (b) The image distance, v, is 2.5 cm, the object distance, u, is 25 cm.
   $$\frac{1}{f} = \frac{1}{u} + \frac{1}{v} = \frac{1}{25} + \frac{1}{2.5}$$ (1) $= 0.44\,cm$ (1)
   $0.44\,cm = 0.044\,m$ (1)
   $$power = \frac{1}{f} = \frac{1}{0.044}$$ (1) $= 22.71D$ (1)

72. Reflection and refraction
1.

As in diagram above: Arrows on the rays to show direction, **(1)** angles of incidence and reflection the same. **(1)** *It is a good idea to write i = r on your diagram, so it is clear that you know the two angles should be the same.*

2. (a)

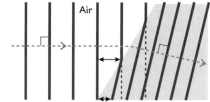

Diagram as above **(2)** with a statement that the waves travel more slowly in glass than they do in air. **(1)**

(b) if the light rays meet the boundary between air and glass at 90° **(1)** *Direction is unchanged although the waves are still slowed down, of course.*

73. Critical angle

1. $\sin r = \dfrac{\sin i}{1.5} = \dfrac{\sin (50)}{1.5}$ **(1)** $= \dfrac{0.766}{1.5} = 0.511$ **(1)**

$r = 30.7°$ **(1)**

2. $\sin c = \dfrac{1}{2.42}$ **(1)** $= 0.413$ **(1)**

$c = 24.4°$ **(1)**

74. Using reflection and refraction

1. Any to from: to check the development of an unborn baby during pregnancy/body scans; **(1)** to break up stones that form in the kidneys; **(1)** cleaning teeth at the dentist's. **(1)**

2. Endoscopes have two optical fibres. One carries light to the location the surgeon needs to look at, **(1)** the other has a lens to view the image; **(1)** light from the lens travels back along this optical fibre to the surgeon's eyes. **(1)**

75. Physics extended writing 1

Answers can be found on page 109.

76. X-rays

1. Energy is absorbed **(1)** as X-rays ionise atoms along their path. **(1)**

2. (a) A heated cathode produces electrons; **(1)** the potential difference between the anode and the cathode makes electrons accelerate to high speeds; **(1)** X-rays are produced when these electrons collide with the tungsten target. **(1)**

(b) Most of the energy of the electrons is converted to heat. **(1)**

77. X-ray calculations

1. The number of electrons striking the target will double. **(1)**

2. (a) $KE = 1.6 \times 10^{-19}$ C $\times 30\,000$ V **(1)** $= 4.8 \times 10^{-15}$ J **(1)**

(b) $v = \sqrt{\left(2 \times \dfrac{KE}{m}\right)} = \sqrt{2 \times \dfrac{4.8 \times 10^{-15}\,\text{J}}{9.1 \times 10^{-31}\,\text{kg}}}$ **(1)**

$= \sqrt{1.05 \times 10^{-16}} = 1.03 \times 10^{-8}$ **(1)** m/s

78. Using X-rays

1. the thickness of the object **(1)**

2. Advantages: CAT scans provide more detailed information, **(1)** and allow the doctors to see around features/produce 3D images **(1)** *(In an X-ray, a bone in front of a tumour could hide the tumour.)* •
Disadvantages: CAT scans require more expensive equipment **(1)** and a greater exposure to X-rays **(1)** than ordinary X-ray images.

79. ECGs and pacemakers

1. Heart rate in beats per second = 1/0.6s = 1.66, **(1)** beats per minute = 1.66 × 60 = 100 beats per minute. **(1)**

2. (a) It measures the amount of oxygen in the blood **(1)** and a patient's heart rate. **(1)**

(b) As the heart beats the volume of blood in a fingertip will vary. The amount of light passing through the fingertip will vary allowing the heart rate to be measured; **(1)** the difference between the amount of infrared light and visible light passing through the fingertip depends on how much oxygen the blood is carrying – this allows the oxygen content to be calculated. **(1)**

80. Properties of radiation

1. Any three from: alpha particles are helium nuclei, **(1)** beta particles are electrons **(1)** and gamma rays are electromagnetic waves, **(1)** neutrons are particles. **(1)**

2. As the count rate is unchanged by the thin card, alpha particles cannot be present; **(1)** aluminium will block beta particles so these must be present as the count rate drops; **(1)** gamma rays pass through aluminium easily and, as the count rate is still above background levels, the source must be emitting gamma rays. **(1)**

81. Balancing nuclear equations

1. The atomic number is 2, which shows there are 2 protons; **(1)** the mass number is 4, which means there are a total of 4 protons and neutrons, **(1)** so there are $4 - 2 = 2$ neutrons. **(1)**

2. $^{226}_{88}\text{Ra} \rightarrow\ ^{222}_{86}\text{Rn}$ **(1)** $+\ ^{4}_{2}\text{He}$ **(1)**

3. (a) $^{14}_{6}\text{C}$ **(1)**

(b) $^{14}_{6}\text{C} \rightarrow\ ^{14}_{7}\text{N} +\ ^{0}_{-1}\text{e}$ (**1** for correct symbol for β^- particle, **1** for rest of equation)

82. The nuclear stability curve

1. Most elements with atomic numbers greater than 82 **(1)** decay by emitting an alpha particle. **(1)** *The atomic number is Z, the number of protons in the nucleus of the element.*

2. (a) 8:6 (1.33) **(1)**

(b) Carbon 14 lies above the stability line, **(1)** so it will decay by beta minus emission. **(1)**

83. Quarks 1

1. (a) uud **(1)**

(b) udd **(1)**

2. (a) The mass of the quark is about $\frac{1}{3}$ that of a proton or neutron **(1)** so there must be three of them to make up one proton or neutron. **(1)** *You could also have pointed out that the charge on the protons and neutrons has to be a whole number.*

(b) charge +2e; **(1)** relative atomic mass 1 **(1)**

84. Quarks 2

1. A down quark changes into an up quark by emitting an electron. **(1)**

2. (a) The atomic number decreases by 1. **(1)**

(b) Any three from: An up quark changes into a down quark by emitting a positron; this causes the proton to turn into a neutron; reducing the atomic number of the atom by 1. **(3)**

85. Dangers of ionising radiation

1. Any three from: A dosimeter is used to measure the exposure of a person working with radioactive materials over time; it is a badge that contains a piece of photographic film; the film is removed and developed at regular intervals; the amount of exposure can be measured from the darkening of the film. **(3)**

2. (a) Alpha-emitting gases are taken into the body through breathing, **(1)** and once they are within the body they can cause a lot of damage to internal organs, like the lungs, in a relatively short time. **(1)**

(b) ventilation using extractor fans/breathing apparatus **(1)**

86. Radiation in hospitals

1. Palliative care is used in illnesses that are incurable; **(1)** the treatment is intended to reduce pain and give the patient a better quality of life. **(1)**

2. Some treatments produce very unpleasant side effects for the patient, reducing their quality of life; **(1)** if the likelihood of a successful outcome is small this is not in the best interests of the patient; **(1)** in such cases the treatment would be unethical unless the patient was fully informed of the side effects and was given a realistic estimate of the probability of benefitting from the treatment. **(1)**

87 and 88. Physics extended writing 2 and 3

Answers can be found on page 109.

ANSWERS

89. Particle accelerators

1. magnetic field **(1)**
2. **(a)** Tracers that decay rapidly minimise the exposure of the patient (and people who come into close contact with the patient) to radiation; **(1)** radiation from the tracer drops to the natural (background) level of radiation within a few days of treatment. **(1)**
   (b) The period of useful activity is short due to short half-lives, **(1)** so transportation time between the point of manufacture and the point of use must be short. **(1)**

90. Collisions

1. **(a)** elastic collisions **(1)**
   (b) both elastic and inelastic collisions **(1)**
2. **(a)** It will rebound at 5 m/s (upwards) **(1)** because kinetic energy immediately before and after the collision is the same. **(1)**
   (b) Yes: **(1)** momentum before 5 m/s and momentum after −5 m/s; the ball has changed direction and this can be seen by the negative sign; **(1)** so the overall change in the momentum is 10 kg m/s. **(1)**

91. Calculations in collisions

1. 850 kg × 30 m/s **(1)** = 25 500 **(1)** kg m/s
2. Momentum before collision = momentum after collision; **(1)** 1 g = 0.001 kg, and 5 cm/s = 0.05 m/s; **(1)** 0.001 kg × u (pellet only moving) = (0.001 + 0.999) kg × 0.05 m/s; **(1)** u (the initial velocity of the pellet) = 50 m/s. **(1)**

92. Electron–positron annihilation

1. **(a)** positron **(1)**
   (b) The positron carries a positive charge (electron is negatively charged). **(1)**
2. total charge, **(1)** momentum **(1)** and mass/energy **(1)**

93. Kinetic theory

1. **(a)** 20 + 273 = 293 K **(1)**
   (b) 300 − 273 = 27°C **(1)**
2. −23°C + 273 K = 250 K **(1)** and 227°C + 273 K = 500 K; **(1)** average KE of gas particles is proportional to Kelvin temperature, so the average KE doubles **(1)**
3. **(a)** The average speed is slower. **(1)**
   (b) The pressure is reduced **(1)** because there are fewer collisions/the particles do not hit the walls as hard. **(1)**

94. Ideal gas equations 1

1. The pressure on the gas remains constant (provided atmospheric pressure is constant) so volume is proportional to temperature; **(1)** so lowering temperature makes the piston move inwards, reducing the volume. **(1)**
2. Assuming that the amount of gas in the bubble remains constant; **(1)** and the temperature of the drink is the same throughout; **(1)** the volume increases as the bubble moves to the top of the liquid; **(1)** this is because the pressure in a liquid decreases close to the surface. **(1)**

95. Ideal gas equations 2

1. The temperature of the gas inside will increase; **(1)** (take volume as constant) so the pressure will increase, which could cause the spray can to explode. **(1)**
2. **(a)** Volume has halved so pressure has doubled **(1)** to 2 atm. **(1)**
   (b) $P_1 = 1$ atm, $V_1 = 100$ cm^3 at $T_1 = 290$ K; **(1)** if 50 N weight has the effect of increasing the pressure by 1 atm, 25 N must increase the pressure on the gas by $\frac{1}{2}$ atm, so $P_2 = 1.5$ atm, $T_2 = 270$ K **(1)**
   $V_2 = (P_1 \times V_1 \times T_2)/(P_2 \times T_1)$ **(1)**
   $V_2 = (1$ atm × 100 cm^3 × 270 K$)/(1.5$ atm × 290 K$)$
   $V_2 = 62.1$ cm^3 **(1)**

96 and 97. Physics extended writing 4 and 5

Answers can be found on page 109.

Extended writing answers

Below you will find a list of points that will help you to check how well you have answered each Extended writing question. Your actual answer should be written in complete sentences; it will contain lots of detail and will link the points into a logical order. A full answer will contain most of the points listed but does not have to include all of them and may include other valid statements. You are more likely to be awarded a higher mark if you use correct scientific language and are careful with your spelling and grammar.

14. Biology extended writing 1

Hypothalamus in the brain; monitors water content of blood; if blood water levels are too low; then pituitary gland; releases more ADH; travels in blood to kidney; acts on convoluted tubule; increasing amount of water reabsorbed into blood; so urine is more concentrated; this means that blood water levels do not fall further; if blood water levels are too high, less ADH is released; kidney then absorbs less water; to get to normal blood water level again; by producing urine with more water in it; this whole process works through negative feedback; and maintaining blood water level is an example of homeostasis; known as osmoregulation.

15. Biology extended writing 2

Follicle stimulating hormone; released from the pituitary gland; matures the follicles and egg cell; in the ovary; high levels early in the cycle; stimulate oestrogen production; rise in oestrogen in days 7 to 14 of cycle; causes the lining of the uterus to grow; and to thicken; when oestrogen level is very high, it triggers rapid release of LH; luteinising hormone; from the pituitary gland; stimulates ovulation; at about day 14; also causes follicle to form corpus luteum; which releases progesterone; progesterone maintains the thick lining of the uterus; so that an egg can implant if fertilised; high levels of progesterone prevent production of FSH and LH; so that no more eggs are matured and released; as progesterone levels fall; the end of the cycle; the lining of the uterus breaks down; as oestrogen levels also low; but falling progesterone levels allow release of FSH; so that cycle can start again.

24. Biology extended writing 3

Mitochondria contain small amounts of DNA; that is separate from DNA in the nucleus; it is inherited from your mother; not mixed with that from your father (unlike nuclear DNA); all humans have similar mitochondrial DNA; the more different two samples of mDNA are from each other; the further back in time the two humans shared a common ancestor; there is a high mutation rate in the mitochondrial DNA; so changes over short periods of time can be more easily seen; analysis of patterns of mutation in mDNA; have led scientists to conclude that we all descended from a single female ancestor; who is likely to have lived in Africa; known as African Eve/mitochondrial Eve; theory is that *Homo sapiens* evolved in Africa; then spread across the world; mDNA is very useful because it is relatively more abundant; because cells have many mitochondria but only one nucleus; and it seems to survive longer over time; without being degraded; so can be extracted from old biological specimens.

33. Biology extended writing 4

Vegetarian cheese; uses chymosin; from genetically modified yeast cells; to curdle milk; rather than use rennet; which comes from animal stomachs; invertase/sucrose; is naturally produced by a yeast; *Saccharomyces cerevisiae*; converts sucrose into glucose and fructose; this is used in sweets; as the sugars produced are sweeter; so the manufacturer can use less sugar; which means that the sweets are lower in calories; mycoprotein; can be used as a meat substitute; made from *Fusarium* sp.; yoghurt; is made from milk; using *Lactobacillus*; through anaerobic respiration; converts lactose to lactic acid; causing clotting of milk proteins.

34. Biology extended writing 5

Gene coding for insulin; is cut from human chromosome; using a restriction enzyme; same enzyme also opens a loop of DNA; called a plasmid; from a bacterium; restriction enzymes cut DNA at a particular sequence of bases; leaving one end of the DNA with unpaired bases; known as 'sticky ends'; ligase enzyme; joins the sticky ends together; inserting the human insulin gene into the bacterial DNA; to produce recombinant DNA; recombinant DNA inserted into bacteria; which are then cultured; in a fermenter; where they produce human insulin.

46. Chemistry extended writing 1

This answer assumes that hydrochloric acid is in the burette – this is the conventional way around; but credit would be given if the solutions are used the other way round.

Rinse burette and fill with hydrochloric acid; remember to fill the air space under the tap; make sure level of acid is on the scale; use a suitably rinsed pipette; to take a sample of potassium hydroxide solution; place in a conical flask; add a few drops of a suitable indicator; e.g. phenolphthalein/methyl orange; note down initial reading on the burette; open tap and run acid into the conical flask; swirl flask to ensure mixing; when indicator starts to change colour add drop by drop; until the indicator changes colour fully; e.g. pink to colourless (phenolphthalein)/yellow to orange (methyl orange); write down final reading on burette; repeat until readings are concordant; i.e. no more than 0.20 cm^3 apart; average to find the volume of acid needed to neutralise the potassium hydroxide; repeat without indicator; and add the correct volume of acid; transfer solution to evaporating basin; boil off about one-half of the water; and leave for the rest of the water to evaporate; filter to obtain the crystals; and dry in a warm oven or by patting with filter paper.

47. Chemistry extended writing 2

Suitable quantity of sulfuric acid, e.g. 100 cm^3; in a beaker; warm and add small amounts of nickel carbonate; and stir; until no more reacts; fizzing stops; some solid nickel carbonate remains; filter; to remove excess nickel carbonate; collect filtrate in an evaporating dish; boil; until about half the volume has boiled off; leave to cool; crystals form; decant or filter; to obtain crystals; wash; with small amount; of cold distilled water; dry in a warm oven or by patting with filter paper.

57. Chemistry extended writing 3

Solid sodium chloride; does not conduct electricity; ions are not free to move; molten sodium chloride has free ions; sodium ions travel to negative electrode; the sodium ions gain electrons; which means that they are reduced; to form sodium metal; $Na^+ + e \rightarrow Na$; chloride ions travel to positive electrode; the chloride ions gain electrons; which means that they are oxidised; to form chlorine; $2Cl^- \rightarrow Cl_2(aq) + 2e$; aqueous sodium chloride contains sodium ions and chloride ions; which can move in the solution; but also water molecules; chloride ions make chlorine at positive electrode as for molten salt; some water molecules ionise; so there are some hydrogen ions in sodium chloride solution; these are discharged at the negative electrode; to make hydrogen; $2H^+ + 2e \rightarrow H_2$; sodium hydroxide is left in solution.

64. Chemistry extended writing 4

Pressure: 9 molecules of gas on left and 10 molecules of gas on right; so fewer molecules of gas on left; higher pressure favours the side with fewer molecules of gas; left-hand side in this case; so low pressure favours formation of product; however, difference between left and right is small; so very high pressure not needed; and would be expensive. Temperature: high temperature means faster rate; so quicker to get to equilibrium; reaction is exothermic; higher temperature favours endothermic direction; in this case, this is the backward reaction; so lower temperature favours formation of product; may need a catalyst to improve rate; if the temperature is too low; need to find a temperature that gives an acceptable compromise between yield and reaction time.

65. Chemistry extended writing 5

Propene is an alkene; propane is an alkane; both are hydrocarbons; contain hydrogen and carbon only; both homologous series contain molecules that differ from each other by CH_2; and have similar chemical properties; and a graduation in physical properties; such as boiling point gradually increasing; series are different as alkenes are unsaturated/alkenes are saturated; different general formula; alkanes = C_nH_{2n+2}; alkenes = C_nH_{2n}; so have different chemical properties; alkenes are more reactive; such as reaction with bromine.

75. Physics extended writing 1

A laser is used to change the shape of the cornea; which changes the amount of refraction; and so changes the point at which rays of light converge; images are focused on the retina; laser treatment is a permanent change to the eye; some people may not want to have operations on their eyes; contact lenses or glasses use a lens that refracts light; before it enters the eye; to change the point at which rays of light meet; the power of these lenses can be easily changed if the person's eyes change; wearers of contact lenses have to make sure the lenses are kept clean; to prevent eye infections; many people prefer surgery or contact lenses for sport; cost implications of laser surgery – the cost of surgery is expensive, although over a person's lifetime it could be argued that more money is spent on the cost of buying disposable contact lenses.

87. Physics extended writing 2

CAT scans produce a better image than conventional X-ray machines; with much better quality pictures/of higher resolution; 3D images are produced by a rotating X-ray device; that produces cross-sectional pictures of the body; nature of CAT scans means that better diagnosis is possible; although the technique does often use a high level of ionising radiation; which can break bonds in the molecules in the body; leading to cell death; or diseases; such as cancer; low-dose CAT scans can reduce the radiation dose; without affecting the image quality; CAT scans are better at diagnosing subtle problems with soft tissue, e.g. brain, liver and intestinal problems; X-rays very useful for looking at bone-related problems; fractures/breaks; or osteoporosis; bone infection; tooth fractures or tooth decay; X-rays can also diagnose heart, lung and arterial problems effectively.

88. Physics extended writing 3

Quarks are sub-atomic particles; that make up protons and neutrons; the composition of a proton is up quark, up quark, down quark; and the composition of a neutron is down quark, down quark, up quark; this means that in β^- decay, a down quark turns into an up quark; resulting in a neutron turning into a proton; in β^+ decay, an up quark turns into a down quark; resulting in a proton turning into a neutron; a down quark has a charge of $-\frac{1}{3}$; an up quark has a charge of $+\frac{2}{3}$; so when uud changes to udd, the $+1$ charge on the proton changes to a 0 charge; and when udd changes to uud a charge of 1 is added to the nucleus.

96. Physics extended writing 4

PET – positron emission tomography; used for 3D imaging of processes within the body; radionuclide or tracer injected (by attaching it to a molecule such as glucose); radioisotope undergoes beta plus decay or positron emission; positron travels a short distance before slowing down and interacting with an electron; annihilation occurs and two gamma rays are emitted; which travel off in opposite directions; gamma photons detected; and processed by computer to give images from inside the body.

97. Physics extended writing 5

The Celsius scale has zero at the melting/freezing point of water; and $100°C$ at the boiling point; the Kelvin scale starts at 0 K or $-273°C$; Kelvin scale relates the average kinetic energy of the particles of a gas to its temperature in Kelvin; a temperature difference of 1 K is the same as a temperature difference of $1°C$; at absolute zero there is no movement of particles in a gas; no gas pressure exerted at 0 K; not possible to reach 0 K; as temperature increases so does kinetic energy for both temperature scales; not possible for a gas to occupy a volume at 0 K.

Published by Pearson Education Limited, Edinburgh Gate, Harlow, Essex, CM20 2JE.

www.pearsonschoolsandfecolleges.co.uk

Copies of official specifications for all Edexcel qualifications may be found on the Edexcel website: www.edexcel.com

Text and original illustrations © Pearson Education Limited 2012
Edited by Judith Head and Florence Production Ltd
Typeset and illustrated by Tech-Set Ltd, Gateshead
Cover illustration by Miriam Sturdee

The rights of Sue Kearsey, Nigel Saunders and Steve Woolley to be identified as authors of this work have been asserted by them in accordance with the Copyright, Designs and Patents Act 1988.

First published 2012

16 15 14 13 12
10 9 8 7 6 5 4 3 2 1

British Library Cataloguing in Publication Data
A catalogue record for this book is available from the British Library

ISBN 978 1 446 90267 7

Printed in Spain by Grafos, S.A.

Acknowledgements
All images © Pearson Education

Every effort has been made to contact copyright holders of material reproduced in this book. Any omissions will be rectified in subsequent printings if notice is given to the publishers.

In the writing of this book, no Edexcel examiners authored sections relevant to examination papers for which they have responsibility.